Library of Congress Catalog Card Number 92-063187

ISBN 0-9623645-2-5

Printed in the United States of America

THOTH BOOKS

Richmond Office:
P.O. Box 29622
Richmond, VA 23242
804-741-4441

Tucson Office:
P.O. Box 85151
Tucson, AZ 85754
602-623-7468

THE DETECTION, INVESTIGATION AND PROSECUTION OF FINANCIAL CRIMES

SECOND EDITION

Nossen & Norvelle

About the Authors

Richard A. Nossen has attained an international reputation as a lecturer in all aspects of the investigation and prosecution of financial crimes committed by white-collar crime perpetrators and racketeers. He has made numerous appearances at the FBI Academy, the Drug Enforcement Administration Training Academy, and other similar federal, state and local law enforcement organizations.

He has developed a variety of investigative accounting training materials for law enforcement organizations at all levels of government. He also serves as a consultant to and as an expert witness for prosecutors in the trial of financial crimes.

He is the author of:

The Seventh Basic Investigative Technique — A widely distributed handbook designed for auditors and criminal investigators.

The Report of the National Conference on Organized Crime — A conference sponsored by the U.S. Department of Justice, held in Washington, D.C. in October, 1975.

One on One Uncorroborated Testimony (University of Notre Dame Law Review – May, 1983) and the first edition of *The Detection, Investigation and Prosecution of Financial Crimes* published in 1982.

At the time of his retirement in December, 1974, from the U.S. Internal Revenue Service, Mr. Nossen held the position of Deputy Assistant Commissioner of the Criminal Investigation Division.

His twenty-four years with the IRS included positions of increasing responsibility starting out as a field Special Agent and Group Supervisor in San Francisco and progressing through a series of supervisory and management positions in Washington, D.C., including, positions related to the development and conduct of comprehensive criminal investigation training programs, as well.

Joan W. Norvelle holds a B.S., Centenary College of Louisiana, M.S., Virginia Commonwealth University, Ph.D., University of Arizona and is a Certified Fraud Examiner. Her background includes teaching and administrative positions at both two-year and four-year institutions. She has taught in accounting training programs for Native American tribes and for the FBI in its Narcotic Trafficker Asset Seizure and Forfeiture program. In addition to serving as Associate Department Head in Accounting at the University of Arizona, she teaches governmental and nonprofit accounting at both the undergraduate and graduate levels. She is the author of *Introduction to Fund Accounting* (Fourth Edition, 1992).

A related interest in forensic accounting is presently served by being a consultant to several agencies in Arizona, including the Special Investigations Division of the Tucson Police Department. Much of this work involves the financial analysis of seized records. Professor Norvelle also works on a variety of cases with Richard A. Nossen & Associates, specialists in investigative accounting.

The Detection, Investigation, and Prosecution of Financial Crimes

(Second Edition)

by Richard A. Nossen and Joan W. Norvelle

Table of Contents

Chapter 5

The Investigative Plan – Phase Two – Execution of Search Warrants   **29**

Chapter 6

The Investigative Plan – Phase Three – Obtaining Information from Banks and Other Sources   **35**

Chapter 7

The Investigative Plan – Phase Four – Analysis of Checking and Savings Accounts   **47**

Chapter 8

The Investigative Plan – Phase Five – Preparing for Trial   61

Chapter 9

Admissibility of Documentary Evidence to Prove Financial Crimes   69

Chapter 10

Interrogation Techniques   89

Chapter 11

Internal Banking Procedures   107

Chapter 12

Illustrative Cases Employing Source and Application of Funds Schedules *117*

Appendix A *171*

Appendix B *181*

Appendix C *189*

Foreword

In the Foreword to the first edition of *The Detection, Investigation and Prosecution of Financial Crimes* (1982), Nossen stated that the role of criminal investigators and internal auditors in government and private industry was undergoing considerable change. He suggested that the value of financial investigative techniques had expanded in the investigation of money-motivated crimes. He felt that internal auditors had begun to question the loyalty and integrity of management: They were no longer merely checking routine compliance with management guidelines but were asking questions about management's personal wealth. He also stated that government auditors and criminal investigators had begun to work together in an effort to pool their expertise. Since that time, these changes in emphasis and overall attitudes have grown dramatically during the past ten years.

The addition of financial analysts to the law enforcement team has enabled criminal investigators and prosecutors to successfully target major money-crime violators. These cases have involved not only the investigation and prosecution of drug traffickers and other types of racketeers but perpetrators of white-collar crime and political corruption as well.

The results of these increases in emphasis and skills, while highly encouraging, are still frustrating. The scourge of drug traffickers continues to plague our nation. The element of greed among perpetrators of money crimes, particularly among those at the executive level, continues to shock and threaten the nation.

The primary objective of this publication is, therefore, to augment the techniques and strategies contained in the earlier publication. To meet this objective, specific cases are described and the techniques employed are illustrated. It is our hope that the application of these techniques will aid in the successful prosecution of money-crime perpetrators.

A second objective, of equal importance, is to create among university students the same degree of awareness that has been achieved among law enforcement personnel of the importance of developing a capability to recognize, deter, and overcome those elements in our society who place greed over common decency and integrity. It is for this reason, among others, that the authors have joined together in the development of this text.

1

Evolution of the Net Worth Investigative Technique

In 1950, which was Richard A. Nossen's first year with the Internal Revenue Service as a Special Agent of the Intelligence Division (renamed the Criminal Investigation Division in 1981), agents of a federal investigative agency, armed with search warrants, conducted a raid at the residence of a local racketeer. Among other things, the agents seized numerous business and personal records.

At that time the majority of government investigators almost automatically ignored financial records as potential evidence when such information came into their possession on the assumption that, without an accounting background, they would be unable to interpret it. In most instances their first reaction was to call the IRS and turn any records over to one of its agents, under the mistaken impression that only IRS agents could interpret financial records and utilize them as evidence. In this particular instance, the records were turned over to Nossen for analysis. A cursory examination of the records strongly indicated that the suspect had been making large personal expenditures over a period of several years in amounts substantially in excess of the income reported on his income tax returns.

A comprehensive net worth analysis of the expenditures was prepared. This consisted of preparing, in effect, a balance sheet for each of the years in which it appeared that he had been making large expenditures. A balance sheet for net worth purposes is little more than a financial statement which contains a list of someone's assets and liabilities for each of the years in question.

> The net worth principle has been used for many years by IRS for the purpose of determining taxpayers' income tax liabilities, primarily in those instances where no books or records of income and expenses have been maintained by taxpayers from which a determination of tax liability could be made.

The use of this principle by the IRS in making a civil determination of taxpayers' income has been upheld by the Supreme Court. The principle has also been upheld by the Supreme Court when used to establish one of the elements of proof of criminal tax fraud, i.e., that a taxpayer has, in fact, understated his income upon which an additional tax is due and owing.

The net worth analysis, which was made primarily from those seized records as well as from limited other records which Nossen had obtained from a variety of third-party sources, clearly showed that the subject had understated his income over a period of several years, thereby evading income taxes applicable to the understated income. Nossen subsequently recommended criminal prosecution for income tax evasion, for which the subject was ultimately convicted and sentenced to serve a prison term.

The same person was also separately charged with violations of other federal laws based on evidence gathered by the other federal agency during the course of their raid on his residence, but he was acquitted of those charges following a lengthy trial. That was in 1951, and the same scenario is still being repeated today.

Application of the IRS Net Worth Concept to the Investigation of Non-Tax Financial Crimes

After these cases, it was difficult to rationalize why most investigative agencies continued to ignore the potential evidentiary value of financial records. It seemed obvious that if the other agency had used the evidence contained in records which *it* discovered as a result of *its* investigation, rather than turning them over to the IRS, the agency would have had the necessary corroborative evidence to convict the subject on the racketeering charges. Why? Simply because it would have been able to prove that he had been acquiring assets and making personal expenditures at a rate far in excess of his income from legitimate sources, thereby creating an inference (admissible as circumstantial evidence) that he had income from *illegitimate* sources.

It was also apparent that most criminal investigators at all levels of government, while not necessarily trained in accounting, certainly have a high level of intelligence as well as considerable "street-wise" investigative experience. Despite a sometimes negative attitude toward examining business records, by not doing so, they were overlooking pertinent evidence which, in many investigations, can make the difference between success and failure.

Over the next twenty years, it was noted that white-collar, political corruption, and other types of financial crime cases were lost during trial because of a lack of corroborative evidence that a crime had, in fact, been committed. All too often cases were lost because of a "one-on-one" situation, where the accuser's credibility was questionable, and the accused was a politician with an impressive record of accomplishment, or a leader of the business community with no criminal record, or even, at times, a racketeer with a glib tongue. As a result, most juries, faced with the dilemma of having no solid corroborative evidence before them to confirm their suspicions, had no alternative but to resolve their "reasonable doubt" in favor of the accused.

Introduction of the Net Worth Concept at Law Enforcement Training Seminars

The opportunity finally to do something about what Nossen had come to believe was a serious threat to the criminal justice system in the United States occurred in 1969, the year that the Law Enforcement Assistance Administration (LEAA) was formed as an arm of the United States Department of Justice. (The Law Enforcement Assistance Administration was renamed the Bureau of Justice Assistance in 1984.)

At that time, Nossen held the position of Staff Assistant to the Director of the Intelligence Division of the U.S. Internal Revenue Service. Prior to assuming the position of staff assistant, he had held a variety of investigative, supervisory, and managerial positions in IRS Intelligence and had gained considerable experience in the investigation, prosecution, and management of income tax fraud cases, the training of new IRS special agents, and the development and management of IRS Intelligence training programs.

In 1970 an LEAA official invited Nossen to participate as a speaker and workshop leader in a series of training seminars for state and local law enforcement officers involved in the investigation and prosecution of organized crime figures. The seminars were to be developed by Nossen, drawing upon his background in the IRS, with no caveats other than to attempt to assist in filling the training void that existed in state and local law enforcement agencies in the techniques of conducting financial investigations.

Nossen enthusiastically accepted the offer to participate in the seminars for a variety of reasons, chief among them being a strong desire to pass on to state and local law enforcement personnel (whom he had always greatly admired and respected) some of the expertise that he had acquired over the years in the investigation of financial crime.

Nossen had also often been highly critical of the attitude of federal investigative agency representatives during training programs for state and local law enforcement officers. Instead of making a sincere effort to teach, the federal representatives invariably made presentations explaining the role of their agencies, how difficult their tasks and responsibilities were, and how good a job they were doing. The result was, for the most part, a complete waste of everyone's time and money which often resulted in an alienation of the limited degree of cooperation that has historically existed among the federal, state, and local law enforcement organizations.

Nossen made a commitment to himself that during the forthcoming seminars he would present to state and local law enforcement officers the "net worth principle" as an investigative technique that they could use in their investigations to corroborate other evidence that a financial crime had, in fact, been committed, thereby strengthening their cases.

Further, he would illustrate not only that the technique was applicable to any financial crime but that, when stripped of the complexities of tax law, it could be taught to and applied by state and local law enforcement officers with relative ease.

Nossen presented the technique for the first time at an LEAA-sponsored organized crime training seminar in Chicago in 1970, and subsequently at similarly sponsored seminars held at Williamsburg, Virginia, the University of Maryland, the University of Georgia Continuing Education Center, the University of Notre Dame Continuing Education Center, and at the New York City Police Academy.

Acceptance of this approach to solving non-tax financial crimes was disappointingly slow. Most law enforcement officers who attended the seminars were convinced that they lacked the necessary accounting skills to investigate financial crimes. However, they recognized the need and felt their responsibility to investigate such crimes because of the alarming increase in white-collar crime, as well as the infiltration of organized crime figures into legitimate business enterprises using capital obtained from their racketeering activities. It was this recognition of responsibility that, slowly but surely, led to a turn-around in attitudes and a strong desire to incorporate this new technique into their other areas of investigative expertise. After Nossen retired in 1974, he continued his efforts to promote the net worth concept.

Development of The Seventh Basic Investigative Technique Handbook

During the course of a three-day National Conference on Organized Crime sponsored by the Department of Justice in Washington, D.C., in October 1975, which Nossen directed under a grant from LEAA, he stressed the importance of utilizing the net worth technique with countless representatives of law enforcement organizations from throughout the country, all of whom held supervisory or managerial positions. They were highly responsive.

As a result, Nossen decided to write a handbook describing the technique in great detail, and, of great importance, in lay terms, stripped not only of income tax law complexities which were clearly not applicable, but also free from accounting jargon, which is equally not applicable. This handbook, *The Seventh Basic Investigative Technique,* outlined in a comprehensive manner how the net worth concept is used in the investigation of someone suspected of a white-collar or racketeer-type financial crime. The objective was to show that the subject has consistently, year after year, spent more money than was available from legitimate sources. As a result, an inference could be drawn, which would be admissible as circumstantial evidence, that there must have been an illegitimate source of income from which the expenditures were made. The purpose of this evidence is, of course, to corroborate other evidence that a crime had in fact been committed. The credibility of the case was accordingly greatly enhanced.

In the handbook Nossen stressed the fact that it made no difference whether the case involved the crime of embezzlement, accepting kickbacks, computer fraud, or any other type of white collar crime, or whether it involved narcotic trafficking, shylocking, arson for profit, kidnapping or any other type of racketeering activity. The only caveat as to the applicability of the technique was that the crime was money motivated. The handbook was distributed initially by LEAA to all of the participants in the 1975 National Conference on Organized Crime. The initial distribution resulted in a high degree of interest by law enforcement organizations throughout the United States and Canada. Permission was granted to the FBI Academy, the United States Drug Enforcement Administration, the Dade County Florida Public Safety Department, and numerous other law enforcement organizations to reprint it for use in their various training programs. By 1981, more than 15,000 copies had been distributed to law enforcement officers and to representatives of the business community.

Over the next five years Nossen presented the technique before law enforcement and private industry training seminars throughout the country, including the Cornell University Institute on Organized Crime, the Battelle Human Affairs Research Center on White-Collar Crime, the National Association of District Attorneys, the Prosecuting Attorneys' Council of Georgia, the Alaska State Police, the State of Florida Department of Law Enforcement, the State of Ohio Division of Crime Prevention, the Virginia State Police Training Academy, the Missouri chapter of the Institute of Internal Auditors, at numerous classes of special agents at the FBI Academy in Quantico, Virginia, and the United States Drug Enforcement Administration in Washington, D.C., and at an International Seminar on Economic Crime, Corruption, and Fraud Against Government, sponsored jointly by the State of Florida, Organized Crime Institute and the City of New York Department of Investigations. As a result of the wide distribution of the handbook and presentations before literally thousands of law enforcement officers and members of the business community, the concept of utilizing net worth evidence and a variety of related investigative techniques was being applied in countless investigations of all types of financial crimes at all levels of law enforcement throughout the country.

Development of The Detection, Investigation, and Prosecution of Financial Crimes

In addition to the handbook's widespread success, several other factors led to writing a more comprehensive textbook. The most significant was the passage of a variety of asset forfeiture statutes at the federal and state levels in the 1980s. These new statutes provided for the seizure and forfeiture of assets acquired with proceeds from illegal activities, and since many U.S. courts do not impose on the government the burden of differentiating between legitimate and illegitimate sources of funds, *all* such assets become vulnerable. Further, most U.S. courts have accepted the premise that when 1) there is evidence that an individual has been engaged in some type of illegal activity that results in monetary gain, and 2) during the same or a subsequent period, that individual acquires assets and makes other related expenditures in amounts in excess of his or her known and/or legitimate sources of funds, then *all* assets acquired by that individual are subject to seizure and forfeiture.

This climate in the courts encouraged law enforcement personnel to accept the net worth technique for its evidentiary value in money-crime investigations, and the first edition of *The Detection, Investigation, and Prosecution of Financial Crimes* was published in 1982.

This second edition takes the opportunity to explore a variety of investigative techniques which have been successful in prosecuting non-tax financial crimes, while continuing to emphasize the strength of the net worth technique. In the next two chapters the authors show the two principal formats used to portray acquisitions of assets and related expenditures. These are commonly referred to as a "Net Worth and Expenditures Schedule" and a "Source and Application of Funds Schedule." In the following chapters, various phases of the investigation and prosecution are examined, and the book concludes with illustrative cases where the techniques have been utilized.

2

Constructing the Net Worth and Expenditures Schedule

When the IRS targets someone for a criminal investigation of an alleged violation of the income tax statutes, the special agent ordinarily contacts the taxpayer in the early stages of the investigation in an attempt to seek his or her cooperation. This approach may not be pursued of course if the facts indicate that it would impede the investigation if the taxpayer became aware of it prematurely. In any event, the primary purpose of the early contact with the taxpayer is to obtain his or her books and records to assist the agent in developing evidence of the alleged violation.

If circumstances preclude the use of this direct approach, or if the individual refuses to provide the agent with the appropriate records, the agent will, in many instances, resort to the use of the net worth method of proving that the individual understated his or her income.

The IRS Formula

The net worth formula used by the IRS is illustrated as follows:

NET WORTH - 12/31/91	XXX
LESS: NET WORTH - 12/31/90	XXX
INCREASE IN NET WORTH	XXX
ADD: LIVING EXPENSES	XXX
TOTAL INCOME	XXX
LESS: NON-TAXABLE INCOME	XXX
TAXABLE INCOME	XXX
LESS: REPORTED INCOME	XXX
UNREPORTED INCOME	XXX

As indicated in the illustration, the IRS agent attempts to determine the wealth of the taxpayer as of a given date and as of the same date in the prior year. In each instance determination of the taxpayer's wealth is made at *cost,* never at market value.

The agent determines the *increases* in the taxpayer's wealth merely by comparing his net worth from one year to another. After determining the yearly increases in wealth, the IRS agent adds to the increases the taxpayer's living expenses for each of the years in question, i.e., expenditures for food, clothing, medical expenses, entertainment, etc.

At this point, the IRS agent reaches a *tentative* determination that if the taxpayer has made expenditures by acquiring assets and, in addition, has spent money for living expenses, he must necessarily have had income.

However, the IRS agent is still faced with something of a dilemma: Some of the taxpayer's so-called "income" may not be *taxable* income. Adjustments must be made to the net worth computation to exclude all non-taxable funds that may have been received by the taxpayer during the years in question.

The adjustments relate primarily to adjustments for depreciation, the non-taxable part of capital gains (in years prior to the 1986 tax act), and other related provisions of the Internal Revenue Code that either exempt or defer income from taxation. The adjustments must be made in accordance with a variety of provisions of income tax law and interpreted regulations.

Most, if not all, of the adjustments are complex. They are difficult to compute and are equally difficult to explain in an investigative report, to a grand jury and, ultimately, to a petit jury. It is for these reasons that the basic net worth formula utilized by the IRS has not been used by law enforcement personnel in the investigation and prosecution of non-tax money crimes.

Once the IRS agent overcomes the problems inherent in making the adjustments, however, it becomes merely a matter of subtracting the amount of non-taxable income from the tentative determination of income, thereby arriving at *taxable* income. Unreported income is then easily determined by subtracting the amount of reported income from the amount designated as taxable income.

The Non-Tax Formula

Recognizing law enforcement's need for some type of corroborative evidence in the investigation and prosecution of non-tax money crimes and the overwhelming success of the IRS net worth approach to the investigation and prosecution of major offenders of tax laws over a period of 50 years, Nossen modified and simplified the IRS net worth formula in the following manner:

- **Eliminated the complexity.** The non-taxable income adjustments necessary in a tax case were completely eliminated; these are not relevant in a non-tax money crime investigation.

- **Placed the emphasis on expenditures.** The objective of the computation became one of focusing on the difference between the expenditures of an individual and his or her known sources of funds.

Once a calculation of total expenditures is made, the investigator subtracts the known and/or legitimate sources of funds available to the subject of the investigation. The result? A determination that the subject has spent more money than he or she had available from known and/or legitimate sources, thereby creating a reasonable inference, admissible as circumstantial evidence, that the subject's excess expenditures were made with funds stemming from some unknown or illegitimate sources.

This determination would provide the corroborative evidence to support the primary evidence of the subject's involvement in some type of illegal activity *and,* of equal importance, would contribute greatly toward the ultimate justification for seizure and forfeiture action against the subject's assets.

As a result of the preceding modifications to the IRS formula, the following formula emerged, applicable to *any* type of non-tax money crime investigation.

NET WORTH - 12/31/91	XXX
LESS: NET WORTH - 12/31/90	XXX
INCREASE IN NET WORTH	XXX
ADD: LIVING EXPENSES	XXX
TOTAL EXPENDITURES	XXX
LESS: INCOME FROM KNOWN SOURCES	XXX
EXPENDITURES IN EXCESS OF KNOWN SOURCES OF FUNDS	XXX

The Modified Net Worth Schedule

This schedule can be set up in one of two formats:

Net Worth and Expenditures Schedule or
Source and Application of Funds Schedule.

The Net Worth and Expenditures Schedule format is illustrated on the following page; the Source and Application of Funds Schedule format is illustrated in the next chapter.

The net worth illustration simply consists of putting in schedule form, year by year, information relating to assets, liabilities, and expenditures. This information is normally obtained as a result of:

- Examination of seized records;

- Information obtained from confidential informants;

- Information obtained as a result of subpoenas served on third-party sources, such as banks, brokerage firms, and other businesses; and

- In some instances, information furnished by the subject of the investigation.

The format is similar in most respects to the format of financial statements prepared routinely by most individuals when applying for mortgage loans.

The principal distinction, however, is the fact that, as previously mentioned, all assets are listed at *cost* rather than market value.

```
                              SUBJECT'S NAME
                              NET WORTH AND EXPENDITURES SCHEDULE
                              1988-1991


                              12/31/88    12/31/89    12/31/90    12/31/91
                              ----------  ----------  ----------  ----------
ASSETS:
-------
CASH IN BANKS:
   CHECKING ACCOUNT              300.00    1,100.00    3,600.00    4,300.00
   SAVINGS ACCOUNT               200.00    2,100.00    7,400.00    9,200.00
UNCASHED CASHIER'S CHECK                                          25,000.00
STOCKS AND BONDS:
   200 SHARES A CORP.                     20,000.00   20,000.00   20,000.00
   200 SHARES B CORP.                     20,000.00   20,000.00   20,000.00
   100 SHARES C CORP.                                             30,000.00
CONDOMINIUM APARTMENT                                 125,000.00 125,000.00
AUTOMOBILES:
   1988 PONTIAC               19,000.00   19,000.00   19,000.00   19,000.00
   1991 MERCEDES                                                  70,000.00
DIAMOND RING                                                       5,000.00
                              ----------  ----------  ----------  ----------
TOTAL ASSETS                  19,500.00   62,200.00  195,000.00  327,500.00
                              ----------  ----------  ----------  ----------
LIABILITIES:
------------
MORTGAGE ON CONDO                                      40,000.00   10,000.00
AUTO LOAN                                                         15,000.00
                              ----------  ----------  ----------  ----------
TOTAL LIABILITIES                 0.00        0.00    40,000.00   25,000.00
                              ----------  ----------  ----------  ----------

LINE 1: NET WORTH             19,500.00   62,200.00  155,000.00  302,500.00

LINE 2: LESS: PY'S NET WORTH              19,500.00   62,200.00  155,000.00
                              ----------  ----------  ----------  ----------
LINE 3: INCREASE IN NET WORTH             42,700.00   92,800.00  147,500.00

LINE 4: ADD: PERSONAL LIVING EXPENSES     20,000.00   30,000.00   40,000.00
                                          ----------  ----------  ----------
LINE 5: TOTAL EXPENDITURES                62,700.00  122,800.00  187,500.00

LINE 6: LESS: KNOWN SOURCES OF FUNDS      25,000.00   38,000.00   44,000.00
                                          ----------  ----------  ----------
LINE 7: EXPENDITURES IN EXCESS           (37,700.00) (84,800.00)(143,500.00)
        OF KNOWN SOURCES OF FUNDS        ==========  ==========  ==========
```

Note: See page 20 for the facts used in this illustrative example and the examples on page 16.

The fact that the dates shown in the illustration are as of 12/31 in each of the years is not necessarily a requirement. It was used in the development of the format simply for illustrative purposes. The IRS ordinarily uses 12/31 since its agents are, in most cases, comparing increases in wealth with tax returns filed on a calendar-year basis. Actually, any date can be used as long as the *same* date is used for each of the years involved. The only requirement is consistency so that comparisons or fluctuations in wealth can be measured from one period to another.

Once all investigative inquiries have been completed the items in the "Asset" section are totaled. Next, the items in the "Liabilities" section are totaled.

> Line 1 – Net Worth is determined by subtracting the Total Liabilities from the Total Assets.

> Line 2 – Prior year's Net Worth is taken from Line 1.

> Line 3 – Increase in Net Worth is determined by subtracting the prior year's Net Worth from the current year's Net Worth.

After determining the yearly net worth increases or decreases, Personal Living Expenditures (Line 4) are added in the same manner as illustrated in the sample.

The result (Line 5) represents the subject's Total Expenditures. The only remaining step is to subtract from Total Expenditures all Known Sources of Funds (Line 6); the result on Line 7 represents expenditures in excess of known sources of funds.

Since 1974 when this formula was developed in the Net Worth and Expenditures format, it has *not* ordinarily been used by prosecutors. While it is technically sound and appropriate for use in the manner outlined in Chapter 1, most prosecutors and investigators prefer the Source and Application of Funds format discussed in the next chapter. The primary reason for their preference has been that even though the net worth computation is relatively simple, the source and application of funds computation is easier to construct and to present to a jury.

It should be kept in mind, however, that both formats are technically correct, require the same supporting evidence of expenditures, and are equally acceptable to the courts.

3

Constructing the Source and Application of Funds Schedule

The decision on which format to use to present the evidence of expenditures in schedule form should be made solely on the basis of which format appears to be most appropriate. The key to presenting evidence of this nature is simplicity. The objective is a one-page presentation of evidence of expenditures (possibly backed up by supporting schedules) presented in a manner all parties can readily understand.

If it appears that a prosecutor has no clear preference for one of the two formats, the following guidelines may be helpful in making a decision:

- The **net worth format** would normally be more appropriate when a subject's spending habits appear to include the acquisition and disposal of real estate, jewelry, furs, bank accounts, life insurance policies having a cash value, stocks and bonds, and other tangible assets, as well as periodic reductions of liabilities.

- The **source and application of funds format** would normally be more appropriate when a subject's expenditures have been of a more transient nature, such as for extraordinarily high personal living expenses, with no indication of accumulation of tangible wealth.

Format of the Schedule

The Source and Application of Funds format is illustrated below:

```
                              SAMPLE NAME
                  SOURCE AND APPLICATION OF FUNDS
                            1989-1991


                                       1989         1990         1991
                                       ----         ----         ----
KNOWN SOURCES OF FUNDS
SALARY                             25,000.00    38,000.00    44,000.00
AUTO LOAN                                                    15,000.00
MORTGAGE ON CONDOMINIUM                         40,000.00
                                   -----------  -----------  -----------
TOTAL SOURCES OF FUNDS             25,000.00    78,000.00    59,000.00
                                   -----------  -----------  -----------

EXPENDITURES:
INCREASE IN CHECKING ACCT. BALANCES     800.00     2,500.00       700.00
INCREASE IN SAVINGS ACCT. BALANCES    1,900.00     5,300.00     1,800.00
UNCASHED CASHIER'S CHECK                                       25,000.00
PURCHASE OF SECURITIES:
   200 SHARES A CORP.                20,000.00
   200 SHARES B CORP.                20,000.00
   100 SHARES C CORP.                                         30,000.00
PURCHASE OF CONDOMINIUM                           125,000.00
PURCHASE OF MERCEDES                                          70,000.00
PURCHASE OF DIAMOND RING                                       5,000.00
PAYMENTS ON MORTGAGE-CONDO                                    30,000.00
PERSONAL LIVING EXPENSES            20,000.00     30,000.00   40,000.00
                                   -----------  -----------  -----------
TOTAL EXPENDITURES                  62,700.00   162,800.00  202,500.00
                                   -----------  -----------  -----------
EXPENDITURES IN EXCESS OF          (37,700.00)  (84,800.00)(143,500.00)
KNOWN SOURCES OF FUNDS             ===========  =========== ===========
```

The illustration contains a listing of the sources of known funds as well as the expenditures for each of the years in which there is evidence of the individual's having committed a money crime. The origins of the expenditures evidence are the same as those outlined in the net worth schedule described in the previous chapter.

Once all investigative inquiries have been completed, the items in the Sources of Known Funds section are totaled. Similarly, the items in the Expenditures section are totaled. The *only* remaining step is to subtract the total known sources of funds from the total expenditures in each of the years in question. The result is the Expenditures in Excess of Known Sources of Funds.

In explaining the Source and Application of Funds computation to a petit jury, the government's summary witness or the prosecutor merely states that the computation can be characterized as "Where did it come from? – where did it go?"

Additional Expenditure Items

The illustrations in Chapters 2 and 3 list only representative categories of expenditures. There may be, of course, numerous other expenditures listed in the schedules if the supporting evidence is available.

For example, in drug and/or money laundering cases, large amounts of currency are often seized at the time of a subject's arrest or during the course of the execution of search and/or seizure warrants. In those instances the seized currency can be shown as an "expenditure" in the year in which the currency was seized.

While it may appear to be difficult to understand how seized currency could be classified as an expenditure, this does *not* present a problem. The rationale is simply that, had the subject used the currency *prior to its seizure to acquire property,* or for some other type of expenditure obviously the expenditure would be included in the computation.

The previous illustrations include personal living expenses in the amounts of $20,000, $30,000, and $40,000 for the years 1989, 1990, and 1991 respectively. If expenditures of this nature are included in the computation, they must be supported by admissible evidence in the same manner as any other types of expenditures.

Personal living expenses are often difficult to prove. Therefore if, during the course of an investigation, it appears that the subject's overall expenditures are substantially in excess of his known sources of funds *without* taking into account personal living expenses, there is no need to expend additional investigative time to prove expenditures of this nature.

One interesting technique often used by prosecutors is to include personal living expenses in the schedule, but in a zero amount in each of the years involved in the computation. It is then pointed out, usually during closing argument to the jury, that even if the subject had incurred *no* personal living expense (a highly unlikely circumstance), he was *still* spending "X" thousands of dollars, each year, in excess of his known sources of income. This approach lends considerable credibility to the expenditures evidence and is impressive before a jury.

One other related approach often used by prosecutors under the same circumstances is to, again, use a zero amount; they then argue to the jury that every dollar that *they* decide the subject expended for personal living expenses, would represent *another* dollar of income received from unknown sources, thereby further corroborating the principal evidence of the financial crime for which the subject is on trial. Some prosecutors prefer to present the "zero living expense" concept to a jury through the testimony of the government's summary or expert witness.

All of the above techniques are effective. They demonstrate, once again, the flexibility in the manner in which expenditures evidence may be introduced at trial.

Sample Source and Application of Funds Schedule

An additional Sample Source and Application of Funds Schedule is provided on the next page. Note that some of the data on this statement for Bank "B" for 1988 can be traced to the sample statements in Chapter 7 related to withdrawals in 1988.

```
                              SUBJECT NAME
                    SOURCE AND APPLICATION OF FUNDS
                              1986-1988
```

SOURCES OF FUNDS:	1986	1987	1988	1986-1988 TOTALS	DESCRIPTION OF EVIDENCE
ADJUSTED GROSS INCOME	$115,003.97	$101,820.30	$276,045.00	$492,869.27	TAX RETURNS
1986 FEDERAL INCOME TAX REFUND		2,647.39		2,647.39	TAX RETURNS
1987 FEDERAL INCOME TAX REFUND			2,853.00	2,853.00	TAX RETURNS
1986 STATE INCOME TAX REFUND		784.66		784.66	TAX RETURNS
PROCEEDS OF LOAN FROM XXXXXXX			15,000.00	15,000.00	PROMISSORY NOTE
PROCEEDS OF CREDIT UNION LOAN #XXXXX		4,800.00		4,800.00	LOAN APPLICATION
REFUND ON PURCHASE OF CONDO			282.84	282.84	LETTER AND CHECK
RENTAL INCOME			7,650.00	7,650.00	COPY OF LEASE
WITHDRAWALS FROM SAVINGS ACCT# XX-XXX			18,400.00	18,400.00	BANK RECORDS
TOTAL SOURCES OF FUNDS	$115,003.97	$110,052.35	$320,230.84	$545,287.16	

EXPENDITURES:

CHECKING ACCOUNT EXPENDITURES:

EXPENDITURES	1986	1987	1988	1986-1988 TOTALS	DESCRIPTION OF EVIDENCE
BANK "A" ACCT# XX-XXX	$83,212.09	$75,178.14	$38,331.81 (c)	$196,722.04	BANK RECORDS
BANK "B" ACCT# XX-XXX		32,205.94	34,336.46 (d)	66,542.40	BANK RECORDS
BANK "C" ACCT# XX-XXX	52,311.12	12,842.68		65,153.80	BANK RECORDS
BANK "D" ACCT# XX-XXX		5,656.90	15,614.36	21,271.26	BANK RECORDS
BANK "E" ACCT# XX-XXX	91,393.72	21,885.46	23,392.85	136,672.03	BANK RECORDS
ESTIMATED TAX PAYMENTS	28,000.00	20,123.00	32,000.00	80,123.00	TAX RETURNS
WITHHOLDING TAXES	5,643.39	6,162.00	7,069.00	18,874.39	TAX RETURNS
LOAN PAYMENTS BANK "C"		24,196.21	50,000.00	74,196.21	LOAN DOCUMENT
DOWN PAYMENT ON CONDO			65,169.90 (a)	65,169.90	CLOSING STATEMENT
DOWN PAYMENT ON 1988 ACURA			11,300.00 (b)	11,300.00	CREDIT UNION LOAN DOCUMENTS
PAYMENT OF LOAN FROM XXXXXXX			15,000.00	15,000.00	CASHIER'S CHECK #XXXXXXXXX
DOWN PAYMENT ON RESIDENCE	66,120.00			66,120.00	ESCROW PAPERWORK
PROPERTY TAXES ON RESIDENCE		2,578.52	3,298.91	5,877.43	TAX BILL AND CASHIER'S CHECKS
MORTGAGE PAYMENTS ON RESIDENCE		24,883.55	29,090.15	53,973.70	MORTGAGE STATEMENTS
KNOWN CURRENCY EXPENDITURES	2,811.69	28,893.28	20,606.67	52,311.64	COPIES OF PAID INVOICES
DEPOSITS TO SAVINGS ACCT# XX-XXX			11,051.92	11,051.92	BANK RECORDS
CASH SEIZURE - RESIDENCE			50,887.00	50,887.00	LAW ENFORCEMENT AGENTS
CASH SEIZURE - GARAGE			225,950.00	225,950.00	LAW ENFORCEMENT AGENTS
TOTAL EXPENDITURES	$329,492.01	$254,605.68	$633,099.03	$1,217,196.72	
EXPENDITURES IN EXCESS OF KNOWN SOURCES OF FUNDS	$214,488.04	$144,553.33	$312,868.19	$671,909.56	

NOTE:	BANK "A"	BANK "B"
WITHDRAWALS PER BANK STATEMENT SUMMARY	$66,501.71	$81,336.46
LESS EXPENDITURES LISTED SEPARATELY ABOVE:		
(a) CONDO DOWNPAYMENT ($65,169.90)	(28,169.90)	(37,000.00)
(b) 1988 ACURA ($10,000 CHECK, $1,300 CASH)		(10,000.00)
NET CHECKING ACCOUNT EXPENDITURES	$38,331.81 (c)	$34,336.46 (d)

FACTS FOR SAMPLE STATEMENTS

Balances in checking and savings accounts and salary payments are:

	Checking	Savings	Salary
1988	$ 3,00	$ 200	$22,000
1989	1,100	2,100	25,000
1990	3,600	7,400	38,000
1991	4,300	9,200	44,000

Living expenses were calculated at $20,000; $30,000, and $40,000 for 1989, 1990, and 1991, respectively.

An uncashed cashier's check was seized in the amount of $25,000 and had been purchased in 1991. Stock and bond purchases include: 200 shares of A Corp. in 1989 for $20,000; 200 shares of B Corp., also in 1989, for $20,000; and 100 shares of C Corp. in 1991 for $30,000. All stocks and bonds are still owned in 1991.

A condominium apartment was purchased in 1990 for $125,000. The amount owed at year end in 1990 was $40,000; at the end of 1991, only $10,000 was still owed.

A 1988 Pontiac was purchased in 1988 for $19,000. This automobile is still owned at the end of 1991. Additionally another automobile, a 1991 Mercedes was purchased for $70,000 in 1991, and has an outstanding loan at year end of $15,000.

Other assets include a diamond ring purchased for $5,000 in 1991.

4

The Investigative Plan –
Phase One –
Quiet Inquiries

In appearing before literally thousands of prosecutors, criminal investigators, financial analysts, and auditors over the past 20 years, the principles involved in constructing the Net Worth and Expenditures Schedule and the Source and Application of Funds Schedule were readily accepted. However, the question almost always arose, "How do we go about finding the evidence of expenditures?"

This is, of course, the key to the successful development of corroborative expenditures evidence. Accordingly, in this chapter we will not only outline an investigative strategy but cover in detail where to look for pertinent evidence of expenditures made by someone who has deliberately attempted to conceal the acquisition of assets and a lavish lifestyle.

There is no perfect investigative plan that can be applied to every money crime case. There are far too many variables that may affect how an investigator proceeds. For example, in the investigation of drug cases activities must necessarily be restricted to covert techniques until such time as pertinent evidence is obtained. Similarly, in a variety of sensitive political corruption cases it is often necessary to conduct initial inquiries in a manner that protects against premature disclosure of allegations.

It is obvious that there is a critical need for a general approach that can be applied to almost all types of money-crime investigations – whether they relate to drug trafficking, political corruption, or other types of white-collar money crimes.

Basic Procedures

The following plan was developed over a period of several years and is still being utilized in investigations throughout the country:

1. Draft a Net Worth and Expenditures or Source and Application of Funds Schedule similar to the illustrations in Chapters 2 and 3. Select the years in which there are indications that the subject has been engaged in illegal activity. The blanks will be filled in as evidence is obtained.

2. Set up file folders for expenditures evidence as it is obtained and a Defendant's Cross-Examination File. The purpose of this will be explained later.

3. Prepare a list of investigative inquiries that can be made without any danger of disclosure that an investigation has been started.

4. Concentrate on gathering evidence *quietly*, in order to establish evidence of probable cause for search warrants.

5. If warranted by probable cause, execute the search warrants at these locations of the subject's activities:

    (a) His accountant;

    (b) His insurance broker;

    (c) His stockbroker;

    (d) His residence; and

    (e) His business.

6. Examine all seized records thoroughly and expeditiously.

7. Based on leads developed in (6) above, and on other inquiries made prior to the execution of search warrants, serve subpoenas on all third-party vendors or other individuals as appropriate.

8. Subpoena the subject's bank records. Detailed information concerning the types of records to include in the subpoena is contained in Chapter 6.

9. In examining all of the above records, and as a result of interviews with all relevant witnesses, continue to keep inserting the appropriate amounts into the draft of the expenditures schedule.

10. Each time an expenditure item is placed in the draft of the schedule, a piece of paper (documentary evidence) *must* be placed in the Expenditure Evidence file folders. The evidence may consist of a cancelled check, check stub, invoice, receipt, memorandum of interview, transcript of recorded conversation, or other similar documentation.

Mail Covers

At the outset of the investigation request a mail cover on all known active mailing addresses of the subject. While it is necessary to make a formal written request to the Postal Inspector in Charge, investigators should also establish liaison with the resident postal inspector. The purpose of the mail cover is to assist in establishing probable cause for search warrants by showing that the subject's standard of living is far in exess of his known sources of funds. This may often be inferred from the receipt of mail from stockbrokers, upscale department stores, jewelry stores, art galleries, travel agencies, credit card companies, etc. It is one step in the process of establishing probable cause *and* it is an inquiry that can be made quietly.

Currency Transaction Report (CTR) Data Base

Federal law requires that all financial institutions, as well as all businesses, report the receipt of currency in amounts of $10,000 or more. There are several forms provided by the federal government tailored specifically to conform to the reporting requirements. They are as follows:

Form 4789 (IRS)	Currency Transaction Report (CTR)
Form 4790 (U.S. Customs)	Report of International Transportation of Currency or Monetary Instruments
Form 8362 (IRS)	Currency Transaction Report by Casinos (CTR-C)
Form 8300 (IRS)	Report of Cash Payments Over $10,000 Received in a Trade or Business
Form 90-22.1 (IRS)	Report of Foreign Bank and Financial Accounts (FBAR)

Copies of these forms are included in Appendix B. The forms contain specific instructions governing their preparation. In addition, IRS Document No. 7171 (4-87) entitled "IRS Special Agents' Money Laundering Control Act of 1986" contains complete information regarding the statutory requirements, civil and criminal penalties, and other pertinent information. Copies of this publication can be obtained by writing to the Department of the Treasury, Internal Revenue Service, 1111 Constitution Ave., N.W., Washington, DC 20224.

Several state legislatures have enacted similar currency transaction reporting statutes patterned after the federal law.

The CTR data base is growing significantly as shown in the following tabulation of forms filed in 1985 and 1990:

	1985	**1990**
Form 4789 (CTR)	1,859,000	7,336,000
Form 4790 (CMIR)	140,000	191,000
Form 8300 (Business)	8,000	31,000
Form 8362 (Casino)	20,000	64,000

Investigators should check the CTR data base early in the investigation of all money crime cases. Requests for this information should be sent to either the Commissioner of Customs or the Office of the Assistant Secretary of the Treasury (Enforcement) in Washington, D.C. A sample letter with appropriate addresses is contained in Appendix C.

This is another "quiet inquiry" that can be made. Its primary purpose is to determine whether or not the subject has engaged in currency transactions in amounts of $10,000 or more. Dealing in currency in large amounts is not the manner in which business transactions are normally carried out. Accordingly, this type of transaction can contribute toward establishing probable cause for obtaining search warrants, and, once again, the information can be obtained quietly.

Government Savings Bonds

Purchases of U.S. Savings Bonds began increasing dramatically in the late 1980s. The growth is continuing and surpassed one billion dollars a month in early 1992. Lack of confidence in banks and savings and loan associations, the significant drop in interest rates paid by most savings institutions, and the relatively high rate of return on government bonds, as well as their safety, have all contributed to this growth.

When faced with making secure investments, perpetrators of financial crimes are no different from any other segment of society. They too are constantly looking for sound investments.

A letter on the requesting Agency's letterhead asking for a transcript of all purchases and redemptions of savings bonds should be sent to:

> Bureau of Public Debt
> Savings Bond Division
> 1111 20th Street, N.W.
> Washington, D.C. 20226-0005

The information should be requested for all years in which the subject is suspected of having committed a money crime.

The letter should include the full name of the subject, social security number, if available, all pertinent addresses, aliases, if any, and, of great importance, similar information relating to the subject's wife, children, grand-children, and boyfriends or girlfriends. The letter should also include a statement explaining that the subject is under criminal investigation for allegedly violating a specific statute.

The request will ultimately be referred to the Bureau's data center in West Virginia and a response is usually received in 30 days. Once again, this is another quiet inquiry, its purpose being to achieve the primary objective – probable cause to obtain search warrants.

○ *Public Records Search* ○

Information is available in state, county, and city records that may lead to expenditure evidence and, as a result, contribute toward establishing probable cause. Since most of these records are open to the public, quiet inquiries may be made without danger of disclosure. The key records are described below.

Grantor-Grantee Records. These records should be *examined* during the quiet inquiries phase, but leads developed should not be pursued until the investigation reaches the overt phase. Records of transfers of title to real property are maintained by all counties in all states. While record-keeping systems may vary, the systems are basically the same. Most counties refer to these records as "Grantor-Grantee" records. The seller of a property is listed as the grantor; the buyer of a property is listed as the grantee.

The record contains a description of the property, dates of acquisition and sale, purchase and sale prices, identity of mortgage lenders, names of title insurance companies, names of attorneys representing the parties to a transfer of title, and other related information. Often the file will either identify or contain leads to the identification of the escrow company that handled the transaction.

While all of the above leads are important, they should *not* be pursued during the quiet inquiries phase. These leads are discussed in detail in a subsequent chapter. The primary purpose of examining the grantor-grantee records during the quiet inquiries phase is to determine if the subject has acquired real property at a cost in *excess* of his known sources of funds. The cost of real estate can be determined in most instances by noting the value of the documentary stamps attached to the deed on the property involved. These stamps are a tax imposed by all counties, usually at a fixed rate per $1,000 of the property value. The local county clerk could provide you with the current tax rate. For example, if the face value of the stamps is $2.00 per $1,000 of valuation and there are $300 in stamps affixed to the deed, the approximate amount of the purchase price of the property paid by the subject would be $150,000. If a $150,000 property acquisition is not commensurate with the subject's known sources of funds, then the investigator is a step closer to developing evidence of probable cause.

Other Pertinent Public Records. There is a wide variety of other public records that are available to investigators. The majority of them, however, have limited potential as leads to the development of expenditures evidence.

The primary records, other than the grantor-grantee records, that may be helpful in establishing probable cause for obtaining search warrants are bankruptcy filings, divorce actions, civil law suits, probate files, and the Fictitious Names Index. All of these have a potential for disclosing evidence of expenditures without making overt inquiries. Through them the investigator may achieve another step toward establishing probable cause.

Garbage Search

Searching a subject's garbage has been an effective investigative technique for many years. While the technique has been restricted in many jurisdictions by legislative action, it should be utilized when permitted.

The search should not be a one-time effort; it should be repeated periodically during the course of an investigation. Unless there are other specific reasons governing the timing of searches, they should be made near the end of the first week of a month. This enhances the opportunity to find discarded end-of-the-month statements from banks, stockbrokers, department stores, credit card companies, and others.

While investigators should use this technique to discover evidence of the money-crime violation, it can also contribute toward establishing probable cause for obtaining search warrants.

5

The Investigative Plan –
Phase Two –
Execution of Search Warrants

If adequate expenditure evidence has been developed during the quiet inquiries phase to establish probable cause to obtain search warrants, they should be served on key individuals, companies, or locations as described below. If sufficient expenditure evidence was *not* obtained, or if the prosecutor chooses not to execute the search warrants, then grand jury subpoenas or some form of administrative summons may be issued. In either case, the investigator should ensure that all of the records described below are obtained.

The Subject's Accountant

The following records should be obtained:

- Books and records relating to all businesses in which the subject may have had an interest during any of the years in which he or she is suspected of engaging in illegal activities.

- Bank statements, cancelled checks, and retained copies of deposit slips on all of the subject's bank accounts for all pertinent years.

- Copies of all financial statements and supporting schedules prepared on behalf of the subject.

- Copies of all federal and state income tax returns and related schedules prepared for the subject. It should be noted that finding a copy of an income tax return does not always mean that the return was filed. Also, in some instances more than one version of a return for a particular year may be found and the investigator may not be able to tell which, if any, was filed.

- The correspondence and billing file.

- Any data stored on or from the computer printouts, disks, etc. (A specialist may have to be called in to download the computer.)

- The accountant's working papers file.

The subject's books and records and cancelled checks may or may not be kept in the accountant's office. On occasion, however, they may be there for short periods of time for purposes of preparing financial statements, tax returns, or perhaps for storage.

The accountant's working papers are usually found in the same files as retained copies of the subject's tax returns. These files are of *critical* importance. They usually contain a "to do" list of questions to be asked of the subject, adjusting entries to be made in the subject's business records in order that a determination of profit can be made, and a variety of informal notes that often incriminate the accountant as well as the subject.

Prior to a recent trial of a major drug dealer an Assistant United States Attorney retained one of the authors to examine seized records in an attempt to establish that the drug dealer's expenditures were in excess of his known sources of funds. The initial examination of the available records did not disclose sufficient evidence of excessive expenditures to warrant the preparation of a Source and Application of Funds Schedule. However, a second review of the seized records led to the discovery of the subject's accountant's files of working papers for a four-year period. The file folders contained adding machine tapes for each of the four years with a heading identifying them as the subject's "personal expenditures." The total expenditures in each of the years were substantially in excess of the known sources of funds disclosed in the subject's tax returns. This enabled the prosecutor to offer corroborative expenditures evidence to support the evidence of drug trafficking by presenting a schedule with only three lines as follows:

	19__	19__	19__	19__
Subject's Expenditures Per His Accountant's Working Paper Files	XX	XX	XX	XX
Less: Subject's Known Sources of Funds	XX	XX	XX	XX
Expenditures in Excess of Known Sources of Funds	XX	XX	XX	XX

In another major money laundering investigation an analysis of one of the subject's accountant's working paper files disclosed notations in the accountant's handwriting with these types of comments:

- "Adjust the gross profit percentage to 1.5%."

- "How could sales and purchases be in an equal amount?"

- "Inventory difference between financial statement and tax return is $600,000.00."

Comments of this type are red flags and their evidentiary potential should be thoroughly explored.

All of the records obtained from a subject's accountant, including those that without exception belong to the subject, are admissible in federal court in a criminal or civil trial of the subject or the accountant. The Supreme Court has, over the years, consistently ruled in favor of the government on this issue. On the other hand, Florida, Georgia, and Utah have recently enacted legislation recognizing CPA-client privilege similar to attorney-client privilege. Investigators in those states or any other that may subsequently enact similar legislation should not subpoena records from an accountant without first checking with the prosecutor.

Stockbroker's Account Representatives

Account representatives at most brokerage firms are paid commissions based on sales. The more they know about the ability of their clients to purchase securities, the greater opportunity they have to generate sales and increase their income. One of the nation's leading brokerage firms, in an effort to encourage its customers to disclose financial information, advised its customers, as follows: "We suggest that you discuss your investment goals thoroughly with your registered representative. The more we know about your circumstances and financial aims, the better we are prepared to help you."

Most account representatives maintain their own files on their customers in which they assemble pertinent information concerning their customer's overall net worth. These files may include:

- Copies of financial statements;

- Identity of other brokerage accounts;

- Identity of bank accounts;

- Retirement plans and location of pension fund investments; and

- A "high-low" potential investment capability.

In addition, most brokers mail questionnaires to their customers periodically requesting a variety of financial data in order to update their files. Copies of these questionnaires are ordinarily retained in the personal client files of the account representatives.

All of the above records are subject to subpoena, or, if located during the execution of a search warrant, may be seized. The records are invaluable either directly or as leads to the discovery of expenditure evidence.

Insurance Broker

Most homeowners and renters insure their homes and/or their contents against losses from fires and other hazards. The major insurance companies cover most losses up to full market value. However, almost all of them place a $2,000.00 loss limitation on personal property. In order to cover personal property valued above $2,000.00, the insured must, in most cases, pay an extra premium based on the amount of coverage.

None of the major companies will provide additional coverage for personal property unless the insured submits descriptions, annual appraisals and, in most instances, pictures of all property to be covered by the policy endorsement. In most cases, policyholders will obtain the appraisals from the same stores where the items were purchased; this creates an expenditure evidentiary trail on expensive jewelry, art works, oriental rugs, etc.

Investigators should make sure to locate and examine appraisal information when insurance records are subpoenaed or reviewed at the time that search warrants are executed.

Residence and Business

Numerous articles and training materials are available to investigators containing guidelines concerning the nature of financial evidence that should be seized during the execution of search warrants at a subject's residence or office. No useful purpose would be served by attempting to summarize these in this text.

However, investigators should keep in mind that financial records are often voluminous and, like all other evidence that is being seized, must be inventoried. In most instances, copies will have to be made. When it is obvious that financial documents bear no relation to the illegal activities of the subject and clearly have no evidentiary value, they should not be seized.

When in doubt, however, the records should be seized and expeditiously reviewed by a financial analyst. If it is determined that the records have no evidentiary potential they should be returned.

6

The Investigative Plan –
Phase Three –
Obtaining Information from Banks
and Other Sources

Investigators should establish liaison with individuals who hold positions in the internal security department of all banks in their communities. Most have responsibility for detecting integrity violations committed by bank employees as well as for ensuring the security of the bank's records.

Many of the people assigned to security are retired law enforcement officers pursuing a second career. As a result, most of them are more than willing to cooperate generally and to comply as expeditiously as possible with requests for records.

When requesting information concerning transactions the subject may have had with a bank, ask the security representative to check the bank's "central files." In this manner, an investigator can determine what the bank willingly discloses before the investigator requests specific records that he may already know about. Among other things, this technique enables the investigator to test the integrity of the bank representative concerning his willingness to make a full disclosure of a subject's transactions.

The technique of finding out from third parties what *they* know concerning a subject's financial transactions before the investigator discloses what *he* knows is almost always advantageous to the investigator and should be utilized in all inquiries unless there are reasons that may warrant requesting information concerning specific financial transactions.

Checking and Savings Account Records

The first records of interest to the investigator are copies of the subject's monthly statements for his checking and savings accounts. Copies should be obtained for the entire period for which there are indications of involvement in illegal activity, as well as for the preceding year. This enables the investigator to make comparisons with the amount of funds flowing through the bank accounts prior to and during the period of suspected illegal activity. Significant increases in the flow of funds during the years of illegal activity often have evidentiary value.

Ordinarily the bank can furnish copies of bank statements without undue delay but may need more time to produce copies of cancelled checks and deposit data. The investigator and/or financial analyst can prepare the bank statement activity summary (illustrated in Chapter 7) while waiting for the bank to provide additional related records.

Signature Cards

Copies of signature cards should be obtained on all checking and savings accounts at the same time that bank statements are requested. Signature cards contain background information, handwriting exemplars, and account activity dates. In the event that a case ultimately goes to trial, signature cards are needed; they are usually required by the prosecutor when he offers the related bank account records into evidence.

Cancelled Checks and Deposit Data

Without exception, copies of *all* cancelled checks, front and back, must be obtained. Similarly, copies of *all* deposit slips with accompanying copies of all deposited checks must be obtained. In addition, copies of all other documents that resulted in additions to or reductions from the account must be obtained. These transactions usually relate to wire transfers of funds into or out of the account and are often of critical importance.

It is impossible to analyze checking and/or savings account activity without having all of the above documents available. Most prosecutors are reluctant to go to trial in any money crime case without having the benefit of this information. One of the key factors to successful prosecution of many money crime cases over the years has been the development of evidence resulting from a thorough analysis of checking and savings account activity.

Loan Files

The information contained in the bank's loan files which are maintained on each customer is of considerable value to an investigator. The files in almost all instances contain copies of loan applications. The applications contain financial statements prepared by the subject when applying for a loan. These financial statements are, actually, a net worth statement. As a result, an investigator can often use the net worth information contained in the statement as leads in developing evidence of expenditures.

Care should be taken to ensure that all expenditure information contained in the financial statements is independently verified and documented to substantiate its accuracy. For example, a subject may have listed his residence or other real property at market value rather than cost, which is, of course, perfectly legitimate. However, investigators should keep in mind that they are attempting to determine the target's actual expenditures each year in order to compare these expenditures with his known source of funds. If the investigator were to include expenditures based on market values of assets, it would result in an erroneous conclusion. It is immaterial whether an asset disclosed in a financial statement has increased or decreased in value since the subject acquired it; only the amount of the expenditure is relevant.

Loan files almost always include copies of the subject's federal income tax returns for at least two years and often three years. This is one of the best sources of available information to determine the subject's known sources of funds. The returns should be examined carefully. If they appear to be copies of the returns filed with the IRS and are unsigned, there is a possibility that the income figures may have been deliberately overstated in order to obtain a larger loan. As a result, most banks require borrowers to sign a letter to the IRS authorizing them to furnish the bank with a copy of the original returns. The copies furnished by the IRS to the bank are the most reliable evidence of known sources of funds.

Safe Deposit Box Entry Records

Evidence of entries into a safe deposit box by a subject, while not having a direct bearing on proving expenditures, may be helpful. A request should be made to the bank asking it to furnish copies of all entry slips to safe deposit boxes for all of the years in which the subject is suspected of involvement in illegal activities. While most bank record destruction schedules provide for the destruction of safe deposit box entry records every six months, they typically retain them for at least two years and often longer.

All banks use a form which contains the date and time of day of each entry and the signature of the subject. After obtaining the entry records, investigators should prepare a schedule listing dates, time of day that the subject accessed the box, and a third column for remarks. Every known financial transaction entered into by a subject where the source and/or disposition of funds cannot be traced to the subject's bank accounts should be checked against the safe deposit box entry schedule to determine whether or not there are correlations between the dates of the transactions with funds from unknown sources and the dates the box was accessed.

Appropriate information should be entered in the remarks column indicating the possible or probable reason why the subject used the box. Dates of known drug buys, kickbacks or pay-off incidents, purchases of cashier's checks, embezzlement actions, bribery payments, down payments on real estate, purchases of automobiles, and similar transactions all lend themselves to being correlated to dates of entry.

This schedule should be retained in the file folder entitled "Defendant's Cross Examination" file referred to earlier. In the event that the defendant takes the stand, a schedule of this type is often helpful during cross examination.

Cashier's Checks

Cashier's checks are purchased frequently by white-collar criminals and racketeers who commit financial crimes. There is a somewhat popular but mistaken belief among the criminal element that their expenditures may escape detection if they "launder" their illegally obtained funds through the purchase of cashier's checks. A second but far more valid reason for their popularity is that the violator feels more secure from theft if the proceeds from his illegal activities are converted from currency to a type of negotiable instrument that can be replaced without loss if stolen.

Cashier's checks, of course, can be traced; purchasers can be identified. However, the investigator must be thorough and make the necessary inquiries to determine if a subject has used the cashier's check technique in an attempt to conceal his expenditures.

Obviously, no bank can be expected to honor a request for information concerning the "possible" purchase of cashier's checks by a subject over an extended period of time. Such a request would be clearly unreasonable and would result in considerable expense to the requesting investigative agency.

Requests for this type of information should be carefully tailored by the investigator to include at least the following potential dates of purchase:

- When known or suspected illegal transactions occurred, i.e., payoffs, kickbacks, bribes, enbezzlements, narcotics buys, shylocking settlements, arson pay-off settlements, etc.;

- Birthdays, anniversaries, graduations, etc., of family members; and

- Potential vacation periods, dates immediately prior to and during the Christmas holiday season, and any other specific time of the year or event that may suggest a need to purchase checks.

The records search has become somewhat less of a burden since October, 1990. Since that date banks have been required to maintain a daily cashier's check registry listing the names of the check purchasers alphabetically.

The purchase of a cashier's check held by the subject uncashed is evidence of an expenditure. It should be shown on the Source and Application of Funds Schedule as an Uncashed Cashier's Check in the year in which it was purchased. It should be shown in the Net Worth and Expenditures Schedule as of 12/31 in the year of purchase and as of 12/31 in all subsequent years in which the check remains uncashed.

⟍ Travelers' Checks ⟋

The evidentiary potential of travelers' checks in the investigation of financial crimes is equally as important as evidence of the purchase of cashier's checks. The same guidelines used for cashier's checks should be applied when attempting to determine when and where travelers' checks were purchased.

The illustration below is typical of the application prepared at most banks when travelers' checks are issued. It contains the name, address, and signature of the purchaser. It also discloses the identity of the issuing company (American Express, Citicorp, etc.) and the serial numbers of the checks purchased.

QUAN.	Denomination	AMOUNT	SERIES	CHEQUES NUMBERED FROM	TO – INCL.			
	$10							
	$20							
	$50							
200	$100	20,000.00	N	276547221	920			
	$500							
	TOTAL	20,000.00	Date 9-15 19 74					
	CHARGE 1%	200.00	SETTLEMENT AMOUNT DUE					
	GRAND TOTAL	20,200.00	SELLER'S COPY FOR RECORD					

PURCHASER'S APPLICATION — SOLD BY

PURCHASER'S NAME & HOME ADDRESS (PRINT IN FULL)
FIRST NAME   MIDDLE INITIAL   LAST NAME
TARGET
HOME ADDRESS

CITY STATE ZIP CODE

PURCHASER AGREES TO TERMS AND CONDITIONS ON REVERSE SIDE

PURCHASER'S SIGNATURE *Target*

After obtaining the serial numbers of the checks, inquiries made to the issuing companies, when properly authorized, can lead to significant expenditures evidence. Copies of the cancelled checks disclose the names of the payees, the dates and places where the subject negotiated the checks, and endorsements of third parties with whom the subject may have had questionable financial transactions. If a subject retains uncashed travelers' checks, they should be treated in the same manner as uncashed cashier's checks and listed as an expenditure at the time they were purchased.

All of the principal companies that issue travelers' checks microfilm the negotiated checks on both sides so as to maintain a record of endorsements. They usually have long-term record retention policies.

Credit Card Records

The use of credit cards has been growing at a phenomenal rate during the past ten years. They provide investigators with a major source of information related to expenditures evidence.

Credit card records may be helpful in establishing the whereabouts of a subject on a given date. This type of information is often pertinent during the course of a trial. While individual banks maintain their own record destruction schedules, most banks retain microfilm copies of customers' monthly credit card statements indefinitely.

Trust Department

Most full service banks offer a variety of "trust" services to their customers. The most important aspect of this service in a money-crime investigation is the performance of "agency" services to their customers. This service is often utilized by a subject if he is attempting to conceal assets derived from illegally obtained funds.

Some of the agency services which should be checked out are as follows:

- Safekeeping – the bank receives, holds, and delivers property on the order of the customer.

- Custodian – the bank acts as a safekeeping agent. It also collects and pays out income, buys, sells, receives and delivers securities on the order of the customer.

- Escrow – the bank acts as escrow agent. For example, a subject may wish to dispose of a piece of real property. He executes and delivers a deed to the bank. The buyer pays over the purchase price to the bank. The bank is instructed to deliver the deed to the buyer and the money to the subject or his nominee.

Trust departments of banks keep complete and accurate records of their trust services and are a valuable source of information.

The above sections of this chapter relating to obtaining information from banks describe the broad categories of information pertinent to gathering expenditures evidence. Additional informaiton concerning other bank records such as bank identification codes, identification of cashed check codes, federal record retention requirements, and other related information is contained in a subsequent chapter.

Examining Real Estate Escrow Files

In the Public Records Search section of Chapter 4 reference is made to the investigative techniques used to identify an escrow company. They are the companies who ordinarly process a financial transaction between a buyer and seller of real property. In this chapter the investigative steps necessary to follow the source and disposition of funds resulting from a transfer of real property from one person to another is addressed.

Once the escrow company has been identified, the investigator should obtain copies of the seller's and buyer's Escrow Closing Statements. These statements contain similar information of interest to both buyer and seller of property. The information includes the amount of funds placed in escrow by the purchaser, the amount of the disbursements to the seller, and a detailed listing of all related expenses paid with escrowed funds.

After examining the closing statements the investigator should request the following:

- All documents that relate to the source of funds placed in escrow by the subject if he is the buyer. These documents should consist of copies of cancelled checks and receipts issued by the escrow company acknowledging receipt of currency.

- All cancelled checks disbursed to the subject by the escrow company if the subject was the seller.

The endorsements on the checks can be used to trace the disposition of the proceeds from the sale of property. For example, the check or checks may have been:

- Deposited to the subject's known checking account, *or* to a previously unknown account;

- Sent to a stockbroker previously unknown to the investigator;

- Endorsed by a third party for some unknown purpose; or

- May have been cashed or used to purchase cashier's checks or travelers' checks.

All of the above leads should be followed to whatever extent necessary in all real estate transactions in order to determine: 1) The source of funds used to purchase property, and 2) The disposition of the proceeds from the sale of property.

There is no need to obtain copies of *all* documents contained in escrow files. Most of them are internal control documents generated by the escrow company, are quite voluminous, and are expensive to copy. The only documents needed are those necessary to follow the money trail.

Stockbroker Records

Most of the techniques used with banks should be used when requesting information from stockbrokers: contact an official with security responsibility, determine what information they have concerning the subject before disclosing what you already know, and request copies of the subject's signature card and monthly statements for the years pertinent to the investigation plus one preceding year. In addition to this information, determine if possible whether or not the subject has accounts with other brokers.

Source of Funds Used to Purchase Securities. After receiving copies of the subject's monthly statements, look for all entries on the statements that indicate the receipt of funds *from* the subject and the payment of funds *to* the subject. This information is usually described in the monthly statements as "check received" or "funds received" and "check issued." Often the statements will contain a series of codes with explanatory information on the reverse side.

Schedule by date and amount all payments made by the subject to the stockbroker for purchases of securities during the pertinent years. Compare the dates and amounts of each payment to the broker with comparable dates appearing on the subject's monthly checking and savings account statements or from the check spread (described in Chapter 7) to see if the payments were made from funds withdrawn from the subject's bank accounts.

After the subject's bank accounts have been eliminated as a source of funds, the remaining payments to the broker take on added significance. If the funds didn't come from the subject's known bank accounts, where did they come from? What are the possibilities? Were the payments made with currency? If so, where did the subject get the currency? From drug trafficking? From a bribe? From a kickback? From an extortion scheme? From an embezzlement or some other type of racketeering activity that generates currency? From unknown bank accounts in fictitious names or out of state? Did the subject enter his or her safe deposit box on or just before the date of the payment to the broker? Did he or she purchase cashier's checks or travelers' checks on or just before the date of the payment to the broker and use them to make the payment?

In order to trace the source of the funds, furnish the stockbroker with a list of the dates and amounts of the payments in question. Request that the broker check the records to determine if the payments were made by the subject in currency or by check. The broker can provide this information from the "daily blotter," a record of all funds received each day, listing the name of the individual from whom the funds were received and the form of the payment (currency or check). If the funds were received by check, the broker can produce a copy of the check either from internal records or from the bank, which will have photographed all checks deposited to the broker's account.

Disposition of Funds Received from Sale of Securities. Schedule by date and amount all payments of proceeds from the sale of securities made by the broker to the subject. Compare the dates and amounts of each payment received from the broker with comparable dates on the subject's monthly checking and savings account statements or in the deposit analysis (described in Chapter 7) to see if the checks were deposited in the accounts. If the checks were not deposited by the subject, what did he do with them? Did he cash them? If so, what did he do with the cash? Was the cash used to consummate a drug transaction? Did he deliberately bypass his bank accounts and use the checks to acquire assets or to make other expenditures that he is trying to conceal? Perhaps he is the *payor* rather than the recipient of a bribe, kickback, payoff, etc. This is an excellent way to provide funds for some type of illegal activity and bypass the subject's business records. After all, who would look for evidence among the cancelled checks of stockbrokers stored on dusty shelves or on microfilm in a warehouse?

The stockbroker should be requested to furnish copies of the cancelled checks issued to the subject. Both sides of the checks should be reproduced in order that the endorsement information, the key to answering some of the above questions, can be obtained.

Other Third Party Sources of Information

No attempt is made to include all possible sources of financial information available to investigators. Training materials that have been prepared in past years for law enforcement officers have invariably included lengthy lists of possible sources of information to a point where their bulk made them literally useless. Many of them appeared to be reprints of a combination of telephone company yellow pages and governmental office listings. The manner in which some of these publications has been prepared indicates a lack of integrity and an inclination to copy old training materials to such a degree that highly obsolete material was the norm rather than the exception.

There are other significant information sources that can be useful when seeking expenditures evidence. For example, car dealers, department stores, jewelry stores, art dealers, motor vehicle records, and other similar sources that, depending on a subject's lifestyle, may be pertinent. All reasonable and logical sources of information should be explored.

There are other basic investigative techniques utilized by investigators that have not been covered in this text such as:

- Physical surveillance of subjects;

- Electronic surveillance when permitted by law;

- Use of informants, particularly former wives, husbands, girlfriends, boy-friends, employers, employees, estranged relatives, etc.;

- Use of undercover agents;

- Laboratory analysis of physical evidence; and

- Investigative grand juries, legislative bodies, crime commissions, and other administrative groups.

All of those techniques, when applicable, should be utilized in seeking evidence of expenditures.

7

The Investigative Plan –
Phase Four –
Analysis of Checking and
Savings Accounts

Checking and savings account records remain one of the most valuable sources of audit trail information for criminal investigators responsible for the investigation of money crimes. The primary reason for the successful prosecution of tax evaders over the past 45 years has been the high level of discipline demanded of IRS agents in the meticulous task of transcribing from appropriate bank records all deposits and withdrawals of funds made by subjects of criminal tax fraud investigations. Over a period of many years, IRS agents have become highly skillful in carrying out this technique.

Most other investigative agencies, at the federal as well as at the state and local levels, have never placed emphasis on the analysis of bank records. Unfortunately, the emphasis, even in the IRS, has substantially declined.

Why then, if the technique is, as the authors claim, one of the most valuable investigative tools in the investigation of money crimes, is there such a lack of effort in its application?

First, it is a laborious, monotonous task to sit at a desk day after day transcribing, by hand, the dates and amounts of deposits and withdrawals and related data. Second, it's a time-consuming procedure and most investigative agencies, strapped for resources, simply cannot or will not devote the personnel or time necessary to transcribe the appropriate records.

Fortunately, there is a solution to the problem. A computer approach tailored to meet the needs of those assigned to the investigation and prosecution of money crime perpetrators greatly reduces the tedium of the task. The use of computers in analyzing bank accounts is not new. The overall approach is being used by a variety of law enforcement agencies at all levels of government. The authors have recently developed a simple computer approach to the analysis of checking and savings account records.

They are presently utilizing the technique in their role as consultants to federal, state, and local investigative agencies and prosecutors. Their subjects range from major drug dealers and money launderers to corrupt public officials and corporate executives.

The first step is, of course, to obtain *all* pertinent checking and savings account records. Ideally, an attempt should be made to obtain *original* records, either as a result of the execution of search warrants or subpoenas. Original records are much easier to read and minimize the time necessary for data entry.

In most cases, however, it is necessary to obtain reproductions of the pertinent documents from the appropriate banks' microfilm records. Banks are usually required to furnish records in response to grand jury subpoenas, administrative summonses, or other similar administrative procedures.

In any event, the following records should be obtained:

- Signature cards;

- Monthly bank statements;

- All cancelled checks (front and back);

- All deposit data, i.e., deposit slips and copies of all checks (front side only) deposited to the account;

- All wire transfer documents, in and out; and

- Any other documents related to charges and/or credits disclosed on the bank statements.

After obtaining all of the above records, the authors provide to the investigating agencies and/or prosecutors the following:

- A reconciliation of all deposit and withdrawal data to the bank statements;

- Summaries of all bank statements for each month showing beginning and ending balances, total deposits and total withdrawals;

- A check spread of all check withdrawals in several formats;

- Detailed analysis of all deposits, including: a determination of amounts of currency deposits and identification of makers of all deposited checks; and

- Identification of all wire transfers of funds, in and out.

Copies of each of the above schedules are distributed to all appropriate personnel including the investigators, the analysts, if any, and the prosecutors. At this stage, *all* parties to the investigation can begin to apply their skills: analyze the sources of deposited funds, make comparisons of deposit patterns with known profiles of financial crime perpetrators, look for pertinent leads to the acquisition of assets, establish patterns of standards of living that are not commensurate with known sources of available funds, and develop audit trails which may lead to a variety of evidentiary sources.

Bank Statement Activity Summary Schedule

Once the bank statements have been obtained, a Bank Statement Activity Summary Schedule should be prepared for each bank account for each year. This schedule is illustrated on the following page. This is a simple schedule to prepare: you are simply copying information from the bank statements. An entire year's activity can be seen at a glance; the total amount of funds that went into and out of each account for each year is displayed.

SUBJECT NAME
BANK NAME AND ACCOUNT NUMBER
BANK STATEMENT ACTIVITY SUMMARY
1988

STATEMENT ENDING:	1/19/88	2/16/88	3/15/88	4/15/88	5/16/88	6/15/88	7/18/88	8/15/88	9/16/88	10/17/88	11/15/88	12/15/88	TOTAL 1988
BEG. BALANCE	2,573.28	594.64	620.83	1,097.59	681.04	671.28	521.28	395.95	395.95	1,561.09	40,070.19	206.78	
DEPOSITS/TRANSFERS	0.00	550.00	1,200.00	1,350.00	10,000.24	0.00	0.00	0.00	3,100.00	40,960.02	18,534.10	4,500.00	80,194.36
CHECKS/WITHDRAWALS	1,978.64	523.81	723.24	1,766.55	10,010.00	150.00	125.33	0.00	1,934.86	2,450.92	58,397.51	3,275.60	81,336.46
ENDING BALANCE	594.64	620.83	1,097.59	681.04	671.28	521.28	395.95	395.95	1,561.09	40,070.19	206.78	1,431.18	

Check Spread Schedule

The check spread schedule is a listing of all check withdrawals and other miscellaneous deductions from the account. The check spread contains the following information in a columnar format:

1. Date of withdrawal;

2. Check number;

3. Name of payee; and

4. Amount of check.

All check withdrawals should be entered – not just those written to specific payees or those for amounts in excess of some arbitrary figure, such as over $500.00 or over $10,000.00. One reason for entering all of the checks is to reconcile with the bank statement, but a more important reason is that an "insignificant" check amount could very well lead to a very significant finding. For example, a check written to the County Recorder for $9.50 could lead to an otherwise hidden asset, a check written to a utility company could provide an address not previously known to be a part of the case, or a payment could be for the fee on a previously unidentified storage unit or safe deposit box. In fact, utility bills paid by subjects have often been used to establish their control over property that has been recorded in the name of a nominee.

Once the above data have been entered, a total should be obtained for each month and/or year. For low activity accounts, a yearly total is adequate. If several hundred checks are written each month, you may wish to show totals for each month.

This schedule is referred to as a check spread because you are listing information about each check in a four-column format (described above) which can then be spread into additional columns. The amount of the expenditure will be spread into columns in order to categorize the nature of the subject's expenditures. The columns set up for categorizing expenditures will vary somewhat from case to case. The check spread can be sorted and printed out in a variety of ways. However, the *first* printout should always be in *alphabetical order* by name of *payee.* When entering the checks, every effort should be made to be consistent in the way in which the names of payees are entered. Checks are often made out to the same person or the same company in different ways: J. P. Adams, John Adams, Johnny Adams may all refer to the same person; a business may be referred to as Puritan Cleaners on several checks and as Cleaners on several others. If you can tell by the endorsement (on the back of the check) that this is in fact the same payee, then choose one way to label that payee even when there are slight differences. In this way, when an "alpha" (alphabetical order) sort is prepared, *all* of the checks made out to the same payee are displayed together.

There are several reasons for first listing the checks in alpha order by name of payee. The primary reason, however, is that it enables the investigators to get a quick picture of *where the money went.* As a result, an order of priority can easily be established to follow up on all pertinent evidentiary leads. An example of this schedule is illustrated on the following page.

SUBJECT NAME
BANK NAME AND ACCOUNT NUMBER
CHECK SPREAD
1988

DATE	CK#	PAYEE	AMOUNT
05/10/88	2242	ACURA DEALER	10,000.00
10/17/88	2266	AMERICAN EXPRESS	414.32
11/25/88	2280	AMERICAN EXPRESS	2,747.90
09/13/88	2254	AMERICAN EXPRESS	148.04
11/05/88	2270	AT&T	255.21
09/06/88	2252	AT&T	134.96
01/15/88	2102	BANK OF AMERICA	1,978.64
09/03/88	2247	BLUE SHIELD	348.30
09/13/88	2253	CALIFORNIA GAS COMPANY	11.31
11/08/88	2272	CASH	5,000.00
12/24/88	2290	CASH	2,000.00
11/23/88	2277	CASH	2,000.00
11/15/88	2275	CASH	1,500.00
11/28/88	W/D	CASHIER'S CHECK TITLE CO.	36,000.00
02/09/88	2121	CELLULAR ONE	523.81
03/03/88	2122	CELLULAR ONE	723.24
10/07/88	2260	CHICAGO TITLE	1,000.00
06/05/88	2244	CHRIS SMITH	150.00
05/20/88	2243	CHRIS SMITH	10.00
09/01/88	2246	CITIBANK	300.00
10/12/88	2264	CITIBANK	100.00
11/03/88	2268	DELMAR APARTMENTS	287.00
09/15/88	2256	DELMAR APARTMENTS	287.00
11/13/88	2274	EMERALD JEWELRY CO	6,512.47
10/08/88	2263	FIRST AMERICAN VISA	720.00
07/08/88	2245	FIRST AMERICAN VISA	125.33
11/06/88	2271	ILLEGIBLE CHECK	120.10
09/19/88	2257	IMAGE FASHIONS	281.36
12/16/88	2283	IMAGE FASHIONS	1,275.60
10/15/88	2265	METRO ELECTRIC COMPANY	216.60
09/21/88	2258	PENNEY'S	423.89
11/10/88	2273	PENNEY'S	857.70
04/02/88	2125	STATE FARM INSURANCE	1,201.55
11/01/88	2267	WORLDWIDE TRAVEL AGENCY	3,117.13
04/17/88	2126	XYZ ENTERPRISES	565.00

TOTAL 1988 $81,336.46

Expanding the Check Spread Schedule

Each check spread will vary somewhat in its columnar headings. Its primary purpose is to categorize expenditures in a manner determined by the investigator to meet the evidentiary needs in a particular case.

The columns listed below are just one example of the many that could be used for columnar headings:

===

				1	2	3	4	5
Date	Check Number	Payee	Amount	Cash	Clothing Jewelry Travel, Etc.	Loan Paymts	Capital Expend.	Misc.

===

The amount column is totaled (footed). The distribution columns (columns 1 through 5) should balance to the total in the amount column (cross-footed). An example is shown on the following page.

SUBJECT NAME
BANK NAME AND ACCOUNT NUMBER
CHECK SPREAD
1988

DATE	CK#	PAYEE	AMOUNT	CASH	CLOTHING JEWELRY TRAVEL CREDIT CARDS	MORTGAGE AND LOAN PAYMENTS	AUTOS REAL ESTATE OTHER CAPITAL EXPENDITURES	UTILITIES INSURANCE OTHER LIVING EXPENSES	MISCELLANEOUS
01/15/88	2102	BANK OF AMERICA	1,978.64			1,978.64			
02/09/88	2121	CELLULAR ONE	523.81					523.81	
03/03/88	2122	CELLULAR ONE	723.24					723.24	
04/02/88	2125	STATE FARM INSURANCE	1,201.55					1,201.55	
04/17/88	2126	XYZ ENTERPRISES	565.00						565.00
05/10/88	2242	ACURA DEALER	10,000.00 *				10,000.00		
05/20/88	2243	CHRIS SMITH	10.00						10.00
06/05/88	2244	CHRIS SMITH	150.00						150.00
07/08/88	2245	FIRST AMERICAN VISA	125.33		125.33				
09/01/88	2246	CITIBANK	300.00		300.00				
09/03/88	2247	BLUE SHIELD	348.30					348.30	
09/06/88	2252	AT&T	134.96					134.96	
09/13/88	2253	CALIFORNIA GAS COMPANY	11.31					11.31	
09/13/88	2254	AMERICAN EXPRESS	148.04		148.04				
09/15/88	2256	DELMAR APARTMENTS	287.00					287.00	
09/19/88	2257	IMAGE FASHIONS	281.36		281.36				
09/21/88	2258	PENNEY'S	423.89		423.89				
10/07/88	2260	CHICAGO TITLE	1,000.00 *				1,000.00		
10/08/88	2263	FIRST AMERICAN VISA	720.00		720.00				
10/12/88	2264	CITIBANK	100.00		100.00				
10/15/88	2265	METRO ELECTRIC COMPANY	216.60					216.60	
10/17/88	2266	AMERICAN EXPRESS	414.32		414.32				
11/01/88	2267	WORLDWIDE TRAVEL AGENCY	3,117.13		3,117.13				
11/03/88	2268	DELMAR APARTMENTS	287.00					287.00	
11/05/88	2270	AT&T	255.21					255.21	
11/06/88	2271	ILLEGIBLE CHECK	120.10						120.10
11/08/88	2272	CASH	5,000.00	5,000.00					
11/10/88	2273	PENNEY'S	857.70		857.70				
11/13/88	2274	EMERALD JEWELRY CO.	6,512.47		6,512.47				
11/15/88	2275	CASH	1,500.00	1,500.00					
11/23/88	2277	CASH	2,000.00	2,000.00					
11/25/88	2280	AMERICAN EXPRESS	2,747.90		2,747.90				
11/28/88	W/D	CASHIER'S CHECK TITLE CO.	36,000.00 *				36,000.00		
12/16/88	2283	IMAGE FASHIONS	1,275.60		1,275.60				
12/24/88	2290	CASH	2,000.00	2,000.00					
TOTAL 1988			$81,336.46	$10,500.00	$17,023.74	$1,978.64	$47,000.00	$3,988.98	$845.10

* SEE SOURCE AND APPLICATION OF FUNDS SCHEDULE

Deposit Analysis Schedule

The primary purpose of the deposit analysis is to attempt to identify the sources of funds deposited to a subject's bank accounts.

Deposits to drug traffickers' accounts usually consist primarily of currency. Those engaged in money laundering operations also deposit, for the most part, currency.

The deposit analysis schedule can vary from case to case. It is usually set up in columns in the following manner:

1. Date of deposit;

2. Gross amount of deposit;

3. Amount of deposit consisting of checks (listed individually, showing ABA numbers and, if available, names of makers);

4. Amount of deposit in currency; and

5. Amount from other sources (such as interest earned on the account). If interest is the only item that the column is used for, then it could be labeled "Interest."

The gross amount column is totaled (footed). The distribution columns (items 3, 4, and 5 above) should balance to the total amount in column 2 (cross-footed). This schedule is illustrated on the following page.

SUBJECT NAME
BANK NAME AND ACCOUNT NUMBER
DEPOSIT ANALYSIS
1988

DATE	TOTAL DEPOSIT	CASH	CHECKS	INTEREST EARNED	UNIDENTIFIED
02/05/88	550.00	550.00			
03/01/88	1,000.00	1,000.00			
03/11/88	200.00	200.00			
04/16/88	300.00	300.00			
04/28/88	1,050.00	1,050.00			
05/18/88	10,000.24	5,300.00	4,700.15	0.09	
09/09/88	2,000.00	2,000.00			
09/15/88	1,100.00				1,100.00
10/09/88	5,000.00	5,000.00			
10/19/88	64.36			64.36	
10/20/88	7,395.66		7,395.66		
10/20/88	15,000.00		15,000.00		
10/24/88	7,500.00				7,500.00
10/25/88	3,000.00	3,000.00			
10/30/88	3,000.00	3,000.00			
11/07/88	6,000.00				6,000.00
11/09/88	2,500.00	2,500.00			
11/08/88	10,000.00		10,000.00		
11/15/88	34.10			34.10	
12/09/88	3,500.00				3,500.00
12/12/88	1,000.00	1,000.00			
TOTAL	$80,194.36	$24,900.00	$37,095.81	$98.55	$18,100.00

Data Entry Errors

Accuracy is essential. Even data input into a computer must be verified. The principal test check to insure against a data entry error applied by the authors is a reconciliation of total deposit and withdrawal figures disclosed on the Bank Statement Activity Summary Schedules with the Check Spread Schedules and the Deposit Analysis Schedules. Footings and cross-footings are additional tools used to insure accuracy. All schedules should also be reviewed by the analyst for reasonableness based on the particular circumstances.

Retention and Storage of Bank Records

After all data are entered into the computer and appropriate schedules are printed out, care must be taken to insure that the bank records relied upon for data entry are meticulously preserved. The following steps are recommended:

1. Storage boxes and "hanging" file folders should be purchased. (A type of storage box referred to as bank records storage boxes has proven very reliable for this purpose. The hanging files should fit into the box for easy access.)

2. All monthly bank statements on each bank account should be filed in chronological order in hanging files and placed in the storage boxes. Hanging files should be labeled appropriately with name of account, name of bank, bank account number, and date covered by documents included in the file. If space in the files permits, the deposit data and withdrawal data for each month can be added to the labelled hanging files containing the monthly bank statements.

3. All deposit data should be collated; that is, deposit slips, "cash in" documents, incoming wire transfer documents, and any other documents that are shown on the bank statements as "credits" should be put in chronological order and filed in hanging files.

4. All withdrawals should be collated, that is, cancelled checks, wire transfer documents, and other documentation supporting amounts that are shown as "debits" on the bank statements. These documents should also be put in chronological order and added to the hanging files.

All of the above described records should be retained for ultimate use by the prosecutor in the event that a case goes to trial. While experience has shown that in money crime cases fewer go to trial than result in pleas, the most successful investigators and prosecutors are the ones who anticipate and properly prepare for trial proceedings. In that regard it should be noted that literally none of the schedules outlined in this chapter are admissible as evidence in a trial until, among other things, the original records relied on to prepare the schedules have been admitted into evidence. Proper retention and retrieval of said records should accordingly receive the highest priority.

It is the view of the authors that the procedures outlined in this chapter are mandatory to insure the successful investigation and prosecution of all types of money crime perpetrators. While it is recommended that most, if not all, investigative agencies should adopt the procedures outlined in this chapter, it is recognized that appropriate resources may not be available to do so. In those circumstances, services of consultants should be utilized. However, careful consideration should be given to the selection of consultants and/or independent contractors. Factors to be considered include:

- Accounting skills;

- Knowledge of appropriate computer technology;

- Law enforcement background;

- Confidentiality issues; and

- Trial experience.

8

The Investigative Plan – Phase Five – Preparing for Trial

When a decision is made to present expenditures evidence at trial to corroborate a money crime charge, the investigator and prosecutor should carefully review the expenditures schedule and supporting evidence. The primary purpose of the review is to ensure that 1) the schedule has been prepared in a clear, succinct manner, and 2) that all items that may create confusion or are in any way controversial have been removed. This approach ensures a presentation of significant corroborative evidence stripped of complexities. It can only be utilized, of course, if the excess of expenditures over known sources of funds is in a sufficient amount to permit the exclusion of controversial and/or complex items.

Preparing the Schedules for Trial

The first two items in the Source and Application of Funds illustration (Increases in Bank Account Balances) are an excellent example of competent evidence of expenditures that, in most instances, should be eliminated because it is often difficult for the government's summary witness to clearly explain why an increase in a bank account balance constitutes an expenditure.

The item is technically correct. For example, if a subject makes expenditures during the course of a year totaling $50,000 and, in addition, has $4,000 more in his checking account at the end of the year than at the beginning of the year, the total expenditures for the year would have been $54,000.

If the subject's overall expenditures in a given year are substantially in excess of known sources of funds, then the increase in the checking account balance of $4,000 should be excluded from the schedule.

The Tempera case, described in Chapter 12, is an excellent example. The Source and Application of Funds Schedule in this case (Item 1 – Increase in Bank Account Balances) shows significant fluctuations in bank account balances from one year to another. The government summary witness (Nossen) chose to include the item in the Source and Application of Funds Schedule. Defense counsel concentrated on this item during cross-examination creating considerable confusion; he succeeded in making it difficult to make an understandable explanation to the jury.

While the government won its case, if a similar set of facts were presented to the authors today, their recommendation would be to eliminate the item in its entirety *if* there were sufficient amounts of expenditures available of a less controversial nature to make a credible presentation.

Presenting the Schedules at Trial

In presenting the government's case at trial, prosecutors almost always first present the evidence related to the actual commission of the crime, i.e., drug transactions, proof of embezzlement, kickbacks, arson for profit, RICO violations, etc. After evidence of the crime has been presented, the prosecutor offers an array of third-party expenditures witnesses who produce documentary evidence and testimony as to the expenditures of the defendant. This is offered as probative circumstantial evidence to corroborate evidence of the substantive offense.

There are numerous court decisions in almost all jurisdictions supporting the admissibility of expenditures evidence in non-tax money-crime cases. *The University of Notre Dame Law Review* article which is included in its entirety in Appendix A contains several pertinent citations of cases. These cases have been supplemented by a wide variety of cases in the past several years.

After all of the evidence related to the defendant's expenditures has been admitted by the Court, the prosecutor calls a summary witness to the stand. This witness may be the investigator assigned to the case, a financial analyst from the investigating agency, or, in some cases, an independent consultant. Some prosecutors prefer to use as a summary witness an individual whose education and experience meet the requirements to be qualified by the Court as an expert (see Chapter 9 for further information concerning expert opinion testimony).

After the witness has been properly qualified by the Court as a summary witness or expert, the witness is asked by the prosecutor whether he or she has heard or read all of the testimony of the witnesses with relation to the expenditures evidence and whether he or she has examined all of the documentary evidence admitted by the Court that relates to the defendant's expenditures. Upon receiving an affirmative answer, the prosecutor then asks whether or not, based on his or her examination of the testimony and the documentary evidence, he or she has prepared a schedule reflecting the expenditures of the defendant. Upon receiving an affirmative answer, the prosecutor asks the witness to identify the schedule and usually offers the schedule into evidence.

Most prosecutors ask the Court's permission to use an enlarged version of the expenditures schedule in order that it can more readily be explained to the jury. Prosecutors usually distribute copies of the expenditures schedule to the Court, defense counsel and, if permitted, to each member of the jury. This enables all parties to more readily follow the testimony of the summary witness. The schedule should be similar to the illustrations shown in Chapters 2, 3, 7, and 12.

The summary witness then proceeds to testify that, based on examination of all of the evidence admitted during the trial with relation to the defendant's expenditures, he or she has determined that the defendant spent X, Y, and Z dollars in each of the years in question in excess of the funds that he had available from known sources. The prosecutor then turns the witness over to the defense for cross examination.

The above testimony is difficult for defense counsel to attack successfully. Other than the possible defenses mentioned earlier in this chapter, there is only one other area of possible vulnerability – the completeness of the schedule. The completeness issue is most likely to arise if defense counsel attempts to show that some sources of funds have been omitted. It is not likely or reasonable that he will be interested in pointing out additional expenditures that have been omitted.

It should be pointed out that the expenditures schedule may not be totally complete due to the lack of all records, the inability of witnesses to remember all expenditures that took place in the past, and the likelihood that the subject has purposely destroyed financial records. The schedule should be as complete as possible with regard to both sources and expenditures, taking into account time and cost restraints. Mathematical accuracy is essential for every aspect of each computation on the schedule.

The expenditures schedule is an *historical reconstruction* of financial events that occurred over a period of years. It is being presented by the government not to prove that the financial crime was committed by the subject but to corroborate other evidence that the subject did, in fact, commit the financial crime.

There is no need to be hesitant about preparing an expenditures schedule due to lack of complete information. The purpose of the schedule is to show that the subject was spending more money than he could account for from his known sources of funds – whether he was spending $30,000 per year more or $20,000 or $100,000 is not the issue; the fact that he cannot point to a *legitimate* source of funds to account for a significant part of his expenditures is what is of consequence.

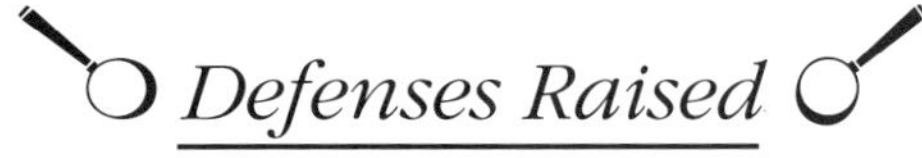

Defenses Raised

In most instances, at some time prior to trial and depending upon discovery rules in various jurisdictions, defense counsel must be furnished with copies of Net Worth or Source and Application of Funds Schedules.

Some investigators and prosecutors have expressed frustration over the years in having to disclose the nature of their evidence to a subject's counsel without their having any reciprocal provision in the discovery process. However, experience has clearly shown that the disclosure of corroborative evidence of a subject's excessive expenditures in a money crime case has been beneficial to the prosecution. Among other things, it tends to assure the prosecutor of the overall accuracy of the computation if no significant discrepancies are raised by a subject's counsel during the course of discovery proceedings.

Assuming, as in almost every case, that there are no significant discrepancies raised during discovery proceedings, what other options are open to defense counsel at trial that may enable them to attempt to overcome the government's expenditures evidence? They have limited options. Most experienced defense counsel will raise the following types of questions:

- Are the government's schedules too complex?

- Are they difficult to explain?

- Will a jury understand them?

- Who will explain them to the jury – the investigator assigned to the case or an outside summary or expert witness?

- Are any of those individuals known to defense counsel? Is defense counsel aware of their strengths and weaknesses, their technical competence, their ability to communicate, their "boiling points?"

The prosecutor and the investigator should anticipate this type of strategy.

Other than the above factors there is really only one significant defense that should be anticipated – an accumulation of cash, allegedly acquired from legitimate sources, in prior years. Examples are cash inheritances that did *not* go through probate, gifts or loans of cash from friends or relatives, and gambling winnings. A variety of bizarre claims, none of which is susceptible to verification, may be offered.

However, it is dangerous for defense counsel to use this strategem. It usually requires the subject to take the stand and face the hazards of cross examination. The extent to which cross examination is successful in discrediting the subject depends, in large part, on the thoroughness of the investigation. The extent to which, during the investigative stage of the case, the investigator recognized the importance of negating future claims of a cash hoard is essential.

The following steps should be taken early in the investigation of *all* money crimes in order to preclude attempts to fabricate evidence or create inferences of the accumulation of a cash hoard:

1. If the subject will talk to the investigator at any stage of the investigation, the subject of cash should be thoroughly explored. The key question is: "What is the maximum amount of cash that you have ever had at any one time other than those funds on deposit in your bank accounts?"

    There may be a wide variety of answers such as, " I don't remember," "What difference does it make?" "Who cares?" "Go to hell," etc. Depending upon the subject's overall reaction to the question, the investigator should attempt to determine through further questioning a more definitive determination. Key questions that may be pertinent are as follows:

    a. Did you ever have as much as ____________?

    b. Would the amount be less than __________?

If the subject is responsive to the above questions, follow-up questions should always be asked, such as:

a. In what years were the funds accumulated?

b. What was the source of the funds?

c. Were the funds reported in the appropriate years' income tax returns? What years?

d. Was the source of the funds identified in the tax returns?

e. Does the subject still have the cash? If so, where is it?

f. Is the subject willing to have the investigator count it? If not, why not?

g. If the subject no longer has the cash, what happened to it? Was it lost, was it used to acquire assets?, etc. Get details.

A comprehensive memorandum of the interrogation containing all of the above information should be prepared as soon as possible. If the conversation was recorded, a transcript should be prepared. The memorandum or transcript should be preserved in a file folder marked "Defendant's Cross Examination."

2. Whenever possible, obtain copies of financial statements filed by or on behalf of the subject. They may be found during the course of executing search warrants at the subject's residence or office or at the office of the subject's accountant, at a bank or other financial institution in the loan files, at an automobile dealer in the "lease" files, or in the records of a variety of other businesses. Invariably, the line provided in a financial statement for listing "cash on hand" is blank. The absence of any disclosure of cash on hand in a financial statement, or the absence of any indication of money owed to individuals, tends, in and of itself, to negate previously referred to claims of cash on hand and cash loans.

3. An analysis of the subject's entries to his safe deposit box may also assist the investigator in overcoming the "cash" claims made by a subject. In questioning the subject as to the dates on which he allegedly received gifts, inheritances, or loans, and where he placed the funds for safekeeping, it may well be shown that he did *not* enter his safe deposit box on

the dates or even near the dates that he claimed to have received the cash. The technique of analyzing safe deposit box entries is covered in detail in Chapter 6.

4. There are several pertinent county public records sources that should be checked out, such as county grantor-grantee records. They contain, in addition to information concerning transfers of real estate, recorded judgments against an individual for failure to pay a debt. Obviously, such a course of conduct, at a time when a subject claims to have had a cash hoard, tends to negate a subject's credibility.

    Other county public records, such as bankruptcy filings, divorce actions, probate files, etc., are equally pertinent and should be checked out during the course of *all* money crime investigations. The importance of checking county grantor-grantee records was covered in earlier chapters.

5. If the subject of an investigation identifies someone from whom he allegedly received cash gifts or loans (perhaps others engaged in illegal activities), they may become the target and face the same investigative perils he is currently facing. He may, by the very fact of identifying them, identify yet other potential subjects, some of whom may also warrant an investigation of their financial activities. This is particularly important if by some remote chance there is a degree of validity to the subject's explanation. In effect, the investigative emphasis could conceivably shift, perhaps to a higher level.

6. There are numerous other types of information available to negate any attempts to explain away the source of funds used to make excessive expenditures. They include a modest standard of living in prior years, moderate income disclosed in tax returns, testimony of relatives, girl-friends, etc. All of these potential evidentiary sources should be checked out if circumstances warrant such inquiries.

9

Admissibility of Documentary Evidence to Prove Financial Crimes

Emphasis in this chapter is placed on key rules of evidence that an investigator should be familiar with in order to ensure that evidence acquired during an audit or investigation will ultimately be admissible in court. Throughout the chapter references are made to the Federal Rules of Evidence. These rules are contained in Public Law 93-595 and became effective January 2, 1975. Since all 50 states have based their rules of evidence on the federal rules, they are being utilized in this chapter.

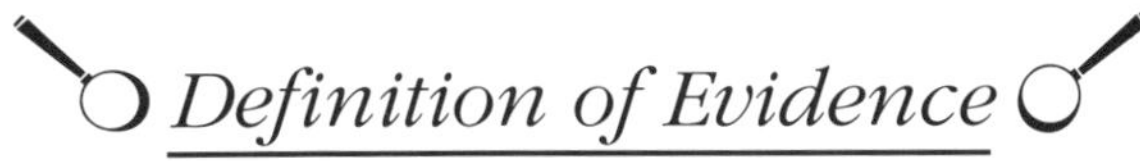

Definition of Evidence

Evidence is all the means by which any alleged matter or fact, the truth of which is submitted to investigation, is established or disproved. Investigators obtain evidentiary facts which, by inference, tend to prove or disprove the ultimate, main, or principal fact. The latter is a matter for determination by a court or jury. For example, an investigator obtains, in connection with an embezzlement case, documents and oral statements showing that a subject's bank balance has increased substantially. That is an evidentiary fact from which an inference may be drawn relative to the ultimate or principal fact, namely, that the subject was involved in a profitable activity. Legal evidence as such is admissible in court under the rules of evidence because it tends reasonably and substantially to prove a fact. Evidence is distinguished from proof in that the latter is the result or effect of evidence.

Classifications of Evidence

Direct Evidence. Direct evidence is that which, if believed, proves the existence of the principal or ultimate fact without any inference or presumption. It is direct when the very facts in dispute are sworn to by those who have actual knowledge of them by means of their senses. It may take the form of admissions or confessions made in or out of court. An example of direct evidence is the testimony of an investigator that he made a "buy" from a defendant charged with the sale of narcotics. Here, the very facts in dispute are sworn to by the testimony of the investigator.

Circumstantial Evidence. Circumstantial evidence is that which tends to prove the existence of the principal fact by inference. The use of circumstantial evidence is recognized by the courts as a legitimate means of proof. It involves proving several material facts which, when considered in their relationship to each other, tend to establish the existence of the principal or ultimate fact. In the absence of a confession to a witness to whom the violator has expressed his intent, violations involving willful intent are proved by circumstantial evidence. Indeed, it is the only type of evidence generally available to show such elements of a crime as malice, intent, or motive, which exist only in the mind of the perpetrator of the deed.

An example of circumstantial evidence is the testimony of an investigator regarding his observation of the defendant when approaching a shack in which he kept stolen firearms, in that the defendant always approached through a very indirect route and at night, with his automobile lights turned off. When these facts are considered in their relationship to the main fact (in this case, a charge that the defendant was dealing in stolen firearms), it tends to prove the existence of the main fact.

Circumstantial evidence may be as convincing as direct evidence. In fact, the jury may find that it outweighs conflicting direct evidence.

Oral, Documentary, and Real Evidence. Evidence also may be classified as oral, documentary, and real. Evidence may be presented orally through witnesses or by the introduction of records or other physical objects. Oral testimony consists of statements made by living witnesses under oath or affirmation.

Documentary evidence consists of writings such as judicial and official records, contracts, deeds, and less formal writings such as letters, memorandums, and books and records of private persons and organizations. Maps, diagrams, and photographs are classed as documentary evidence. Real or physical evidence (sometimes called demonstrative evidence) relates to tangible objects or property, such as a knife or pistol, which are admitted in court or inspected by a trier of facts.

Relevancy, Materiality, and Competency

To be admissible, evidence must be relevant, material, and competent.

Relevancy. If a fact offered in evidence relates in some logical way to the principal fact, it is relevant. The word "relevant" implies a traceable and significant connection. A fact need not bear directly on the principal fact. It is sufficient if it constitutes one link in a chain of evidence or if it relates to facts which would constitute circumstantial evidence that a fact in issue did or did not exist. One fact is logically relevant to another if, taken by itself or in connection with other facts, it proves or tends to prove the existence of the other fact. If the fact is logically relevant, it is also legally relevant unless it is barred by some rule of evidence.

Rule 401 of the Federal Rules of Evidence (hereafter referred to as F.R.E.) defines relevant evidence as *"...evidence having any tendency to make the existence of any fact that is of consequence to the determination of the action more probable or less probable than it would be without the evidence."* Rule 402 provides that "all relevant evidence is admissible, except as otherwise provided by the Constitution of the United States, by Act of Congress, or by other rules prescribed by the Supreme Court pursuant to statutory authority. Evidence which is not relevant is not admissible."

Investigators should obtain and report all facts which logically relate to the subject of the investigation. They should not omit any significant facts because of doubt regarding their relevance. There are no absolute and concrete standards for relevancy because the facts vary in each case and judges have broad discretion in determining what evidence is relevant. Similarly, the investigator should not omit evidence because of doubt as to its materiality or competency.

Materiality. Under F.R.E., materiality is no longer a criterion. Heretofore, evidence was considered to be material if it tended to cast light on the subject in dispute, to affect the outcome of the trial, or to help establish the guilt or innocence of the accused. This definition is now included in the definition of relevancy (Rule 401 above).

Competency. The terms "relevant" and "competent" are not synonymous. Evidence must not only be logically relevant and sufficiently persuasive but also legally admissible, in other words, competent. Relevant evidence may be incompetent and hence inadmissible because it is hearsay, or not the best evidence.

The words "irrelevant" and "immaterial" usually refer more particularly to the statement one is seeking to elicit. Although incompetency may relate to documents, in many cases it may refer to the person or the witness in that he may suffer some disability which prevents him from testifying in the particular case. For example, a person is not competent to testify if he does not understand the nature of an oath or is unable to narrate with understanding the facts he has seen.

As applied to evidence such as documents, evidence is competent if it was obtained in a manner, in a form, and from a source proper under the law. Examples of incompetent evidence are a confession involuntarily obtained or an unsigned carbon copy of a document which is offered without any explanation for the failure to produce the original.

Limited Admissibility. Evidence may have limited admissibility. The fact that certain evidence is not admissible for one purpose does not preclude its use for another. An evidentiary fact may not be admissible as independent proof of the principal fact and yet be admitted to corroborate or impeach.

Hearsay

Hearsay has been defined as evidence which does not come from the personal knowledge of the witness but from the mere repetition of what he has heard others say. It also relates to the offering by a witness of a document prepared by another person. Hearsay is secondhand evidence and is generally excluded. An investigator's testimony that payees of corporate checks have told him the checks were for personal expenses of the subject, an officer of the corporation, is inadmissible as hearsay. The personal nature of the payments should be proven through the subject's own records, testimony of the investigator or others as to his admissions, or testimony of third parties.

Lack of opportunity for cross-examination is the principal reason for excluding hearsay testimony. As stated in the Papadakis case: *The hearsay rule is concerned only with the reliability of evidence offered to prove a fact, whatever that fact might be. It operates to render inadmissible extra-judicial writings or declarations introduced to prove the truth of what was said or written, on the theory that such evidence, not being subject to the tests of cross-examination, is not reliable. 5 Wigmore on Evidence, 1361.*

Cross-examination is essential as a test of the truth of the facts offered. It provides an opportunity to test the credibility of the witness, his observations, memory, bias, prejudice, and possible errors. It also subjects the witness to the penalties of perjury and may eliminate deliberate or unintentional misstatements of what he has been told.

Admissions and Confessions. Under the Federal Rules of Evidence, an admission is not considered to be hearsay. An admission may be defined as a statement or act of a party which is offered in evidence against him (F.R.E. 801). It also may be defined as a prior oral or written statement or act of a party which is inconsistent with his position in the pleadings or at the trial. Admissions can be used either as evidence of facts or to discredit a party as a witness. They can be used only as to facts, not as to matters of law, opinion, or hearsay. A confession is a statement of a person that he is guilty of a crime.

Exceptions to Hearsay Rule. The courts, in the interest of justice, have made certain exceptions to the hearsay rule. The exceptions are based on two principal reasons: necessity for use and probability of trustworthiness. The so-called necessity rule usually comes into being because the person who made the statement would be unavailable to appear and testify, and the court would thereby be deprived of evidence that is important in the decision of an issue. In addition to being necessary, the evidence must also have the probability of truthfulness that will substitute for cross-examination. Evidence that meets the above standards is admissible as an exception to the hearsay rule. Some of the more important exceptions are:

1. Business Records, Public Records and Commercial Documents. Records containing entries made in the regular course of business, as well as marriage, baptismal, and similar certificates, are admissible without the testimony of the person who made the entries, if they are properly identified by some witness. Public records made by an officer in the performance of his duties are also admissible after proper authentication.

2. Expert and Opinion Testimony. Expert opinions are the conclusions of a person who has been qualified as an expert in his field; they are admitted to aid the jury in its deliberations. Opinions of laymen may also be admitted into evidence under certain circumstances, e.g., handwriting recognition and physical condition. As another example, a police officer may give his opinion concerning the speed of an automobile. The basis for permitting this is that the police officer has specialized experience beyond that of the ordinary person, which would qualify him to give his opinion of the matter.

3. Reputation. A defendant in a prosecution may offer witnesses to testify to his good reputation in the community where he lives. Such evidence is competent because it may tend to generate a reasonable doubt of his guilt. The evidence should be restricted to the character trait in issue and should bear an analogy to the nature of the charge. For instance, a witness for the defendant in a bribery case may be asked on direct examination if he knows the defendant's general reputation for truth and veracity in the community, whereas a question about his reputation for peacefulness would be improper. The witnesses must confine their testimony to general reputation and may not testify about their own knowledge or observation of the defendant, or about his specific acts or courses of conduct. Once the defense has raised the issue of character, the prosecution may offer evidence of bad reputation in rebuttal of character testimony. Rule 405, F.R.E., provides that *"on cross-examination inquiry is allowable into relevant specific instances of conduct"*.

4. Records of Documents Affecting an Interest in Property. If a document affecting an interest in property (e.g., a deed) is recorded in a public office and an applicable statute authorizes the recording of documents of that kind in that office, the record of such document may be admissible as proof of the original recorded document and its execution and delivery by each person by whom it is purported to have been executed (F.R.E. 803 [14]).

5. Mental and Physical Condition. Contemporaneous or spontaneous declarations of a person may be admissible to prove his mental or physical condition. While such statements carry more weight when made to a physician for purposes of treatment, they may be competent even if made to family members or to other persons. Thus, a trial court in a fraud case might admit a lay witness's testimony that he heard the defendant complain of severe headaches and inability to concentrate just before preparing his alleged false travel expense voucher.

6. Excited Utterance (Also Known as "Spontaneous Declaration"). This has been defined as *"a statement relating to a startling event or condition made while the declarant was under the stress or excitement caused by the event or condition"*. (F.R.E. 803 [2]). The trustworthiness of such statements lies in their spontaneity, for the occurrence must be startling enough to produce a spontaneous and unreflected utterance without time to contrive or to misrepresent.

Excited utterances may be made by participants or by bystanders, and a person who made or heard such statements may testify about them in court.

7. Recorded Recollection. A memorandum or record about which a witness once had knowledge, but about which at the time he is called to testify he has insufficient recollection to enable him to testify fully and accurately may be used in court. It must be shown, however, that the memorandum or record was made or adopted by the witness when the matter was fresh in his memory and reflects his knowledge correctly. If admitted, the memorandum or record may be read into evidence, but may not itself be received as an exhibit unless offered by an adverse party (F.R.E. 803 [5]).

8. Absence of Entry. The Federal Rules of Evidence also provide for an exception to the hearsay rule with respect to evidence of the absence of an entry in records kept in the regular course of business and absence of a public record or entry if the matter was of a kind in which the business or public office ordinarily made and perserved a record. It must be shown that a diligent search of the records has been made, and the evidence may be ruled inadmissible if "the sources of information or other circumstances indicate lack of trustworthiness" (F.R.E. 803 [7] and [10]).

9. Hearsay Exceptions: Declarant Unavailable. The following exceptions to the hearsay rule relate to situations in which the declarant (person who made the statement) is unavailable for the trial (for example, if he has died, has disappeared, is mentally or physically incapacitated, is beyond the jurisdiction of the court, or is exempted by ruling of the court on the ground of privilege concerning the subject matter of his statement):

a. Former Testimony. *"Testimony given as a witness at another hearing of the same or a different proceeding, or in a deposition taken in compliance with law in the course of the same or another proceeding, if the party against whom the testimony is now offered (in a criminal proceeding) had an opportunity and similar motive to develop the testimony by direct, cross or redirect examination"* (F.R.E. 804 (b) [1]). [Parenthetical element supplied]

b. Statement Against Interest. A statement against interest relates to an oral or written declaration by one not a party to the action and not available to testify. It must be shown that such statement was, at the time of its making, so far contrary to the declarant's pecuniary or proprietary interest, or so far tended to make invalid a claim by him against another, that a reasonable person in his position would not have made the statement unless he believed it to be true. For example, in order to establish that a defendant paid off a large debt with currency on a certain date, the government may prove the payment through an entry in the personal diary of the deceased creditor. The diary could be identified by a relative of the deceased as having been found among his papers after his death. The Federal Rules of Evidence (804 (b) (3)) and some courts have extended this rule to include statements against penal interest.

c. Dying Declarations. Dying declarations are statements made by the victim of a homicide who believes that death is imminent. To be admissible, such statements must relate only to facts concerning the cause for and circumstances surrounding the homicide charged. They are admitted from the necessities of the case to prevent a failure of justice. Furthermore, the sense of impending death is presumed to remove all temptation of falsehood. The statements may be admitted only in the murder trial, or under Rule 804 (b) [2], in a civil proceeding.

Documentary Evidence

Documentary evidence is evidence consisting of writings and documents as distinguished from parol, that is, oral evidence.

Best Evidence Rule. The best evidence rule, which applies only to documentary evidence, is that the best proof of the contents of a document is the document itself. The best evidence rule, requiring production of the original document, is confined to cases where it is sought to prove the contents of the document. Production consists of either making the writing available to the judge and the counsel for the adversary or having it read aloud in open court. Facts about a document other than its contents are provable without its production. For example, the fact that a sales contract was made is a fact separate from the actual terms of the contract and may be proven by testimony alone.

Traditionally, the best evidence rule applied essentially to documents. However, current techniques of storing data have dictated its expansion to include computers, photographic systems, and other developments. In the Federal Rules of Evidence (Rule 1001) writings and recordings are defined as "letters, words or numbers, or their equivalent, set down by handwriting, typewriting, printing, photostating, photographing, magnetic impulse, mechanical or electrical recording, or other form of data compilation." The original of a writing or recording is defined as "the writing or recording itself or any counterpart intended to have the same effect by a person executing or issuing it."

Certain documents, such as leases, contracts or even letters, which are executed (signed) in more than one copy are all considered originals, and any one of the copies may be produced as an original.

Application of Best Evidence Rule. When an original document is not produced and its absence is satisfactorily explained, secondary evidence, which could consist of testimony of witnesses or a copy of the writing, will be received to prove its contents. Unavailability of the original document is a question to be decided by the trial judge, just as he decides all questions regarding admissibility of evidence.

The reason for the rule is to prevent fraud, mistake, or error. For example, the testimony of an investigator as to the contents of a sales invoice will be excluded unless it is shown that the invoice itself is unavailable. However, in that event, the investigator's testimony is admissible, even though the person who prepared the invoice is available to testify. The best evidence rule will not be invoked to exclude oral testimony of one witness merely because another witness could give more conclusive testimony.

Secondary Evidence.   All evidence falling short of the standard for best evidence is classed as secondary evidence and is a substitute for better evidence. Stated in another way, when it is shown from the face of the evidence itself or by other proof that better evidence was or is available, the evidence is classified as secondary evidence.

Secondary evidence may be either the testimony of witnesses or a copy of the writing. There is no settled rule stating which of these is a higher degree of secondary evidence.

Before secondary evidence of any nature may be admitted, there must be satisfactory evidence of the present or former existence of an original document, properly executed and genuine. It must be established that the original has been destroyed, lost, stolen, or is otherwise unavailable. In all cases, except destruction provable by an eyewitness, the party proving the document must have used all reasonable means to obtain the original; that is, he must have made such diligent search as was reasonable under the facts. Some cases have specifically set the rule that search must be made in the place where the document was last known to be, or that inquiry must be made of the person who last had custody of it. In every case, the sufficiency of the search is a matter to be determined by the court. If a document is offered as secondary evidence, it must be shown to be a correct copy of the original to be admissible.

When the original document has been destroyed by the party attempting to prove its contents, secondary evidence of the contents will be admitted if the destruction was in the ordinary course of business, or by mistake, or even intentionally, provided it was not done for any fraudulent purpose.

With respect to an original document in the possession of an opponent, Rule 1004, F.R.E., provides that the original is not required and that other evidence of the contents is admissible if, at the time the original was under the control of the party against whom offered, he was put on notice by the pleadings or otherwise that the contents would be subject to proof at the hearing and he does not produce the original at the hearing.

Admissibility of Documentary Evidence

Records of Regularly Conducted (Business) Activity. Rule 803 [6], F.R.E., states: *"A memorandum, report, record, or data compilation, in any form, of acts, events, conditions, opinions, or diagnoses, made at or near the time by, or from information transmitted by, a person with knowledge, if kept in the course of a regularly conducted business activity, and if it was the regular practice of that business activity to make the memorandum, report, record, or data compilation, all as shown by the testimony of the custodian or other qualified witness, unless the source of information or the method or circumstances of preparation indicate lack of trustworthiness, is admissible. The term 'business' as used in this paragraph includes business, institution, association, profession, occupation, and calling of every kind, whether or not conducted for profit."*

The above rule permits showing that an entry was made in a book maintained in the regular course of business without producing the particular person who made the entry and having him identify it. For example, in proving a sale, an employee of the customer may appear with the original purchase journal and cash disbursements book of the customer and testify that these were books of original entry showing purchases by the customer, even though the witness is not the person who made the entries.

The essence of the "regular course of business" rule is the reliance on records made under circumstances showing no reason or motive to misrepresent the facts. As stated by the courts, "The rule contemplates that certain events are regularly recorded as 'routine reflections of the day-to-day operations of a business' so that the 'character of the records and their earmarks of reliability' import trustworthiness". For example, the rule is applied to bank records under the theory that the accuracy of the records is essential to the very life of the bank's business.

The mere fact that a record has been kept in the regular course of business is not of itself enough to make it admissible. The rules of competency and relevancy must still be applied, as for any other evidence. If a ledger is offered in evidence to prove entries posted from a journal which is available, the journal itself, as the book of original entry, should be produced.

When, in the regular course of business, it is the practice to photograph, photostat, or microfilm the business records mentioned above, such reproductions, when satisfactorily identified, are as admissible as the original. Similarly, enlargements of the original reproductions are admissible if the original reproduction is in existence and available for inspection under the direction of the court. This rule is particularly helpful in connection with bank records because of the common practice of microfilming ledger sheets, deposit tickets, and checks.

Photographs, Photostats, and Microfilmed Copies. Photographs, photostats, and microfilmed copies of writings *not* made in the regular course of business are considered secondary evidence of the contents, generally inadmissible if the original can be produced and no reason is given for failure to produce it. The same rule is usually applied where the original is already in evidence and no reason has been given for offering the copy. However, notes of the Advisory Committee regarding the Federal Rules of Evidence indicate an intent to liberalize the rule with respect to photostatic copies to the extent that such copies may be admitted in evidence in absence of a showing of some reason for requiring the original (Rule 1003).

A photographic or photostatic reproduction of a document may be admitted after evidence has been produced that the original cannot be obtained and that the reproduction is an exact and accurate copy. This principle has been followed where the original was in the hands of the defendant and its production could not be compelled by the government. It has further been held that a photograph of a promissory note taken because the writing was becoming faded and illegible was admissible in place of the illegible original.

When photostats of documents are obtained during an investigation, they should be initialed on the back, after comparison with the original, by the one who made the photostat or by the investigator who obtained the document which was photostated. The date of such comparison should be noted following the initial. The source of the original document should be set out on the reverse of the photostat or on an initialed attachment or memorandum relating to each photostat or group of photostats covered by the one memorandum. This procedure will ensure proper authentication at a trial.

Transcripts.   Transcripts are copies of writings and are admissible as secondary evidence under the same principles governing the admission of photographs or photostatic reproductions. An investigator should take certain precautions in the preparation of transcripts to ensure proper authentication for their admission at a trial when the original documents are unavailable. He should carefully compare the transcript with the original and certify that it is a correct transcript. The certification should show the date that the transcript was made, by whom and where it was made, and the source from which it was taken. Each page should be identified by the investigator to show that it forms part of the whole. A good practice is to show the total number of pages involved, as, page 1 of 5 pages. When a partial transcript is made, it should be so indicated, for example, "excerpt from page 5 of the cash receipts book".

Charts, Schedules and Summaries.   Charts, schedules, and summaries prepared by investigators may be placed in evidence at the discretion of the court if they are summaries of evidence previously admitted in a case. This is permitted as a matter of convenience to the court and jury. At times such charts, summaries, and schedules have been permitted in the jury room to aid in the jury's deliberations.

Schedules may be used to summarize specific business transactions. For example, in one case involving the purchase and resale of 202 used automobiles, a schedule of those items showing the details of the transactions was admitted into evidence after the introduction of the pertinent records and testimony.

Care should be exercised, however, in the preparation of charts, summaries, and schedules to avoid prejudicial headings or titles. For example, a chart listing a series of false entries on an expense voucher should *not* be entitled "fraudulent entries."

Notes, Diaries, Workpapers, and Memorandums.   Notes, diaries, workpapers, and memorandums made by auditors during an investigation ordinarily are not considered evidence. However, they may be used on the witness stand or prior to testifying as an aid to recollection or may be introduced into evidence by the adverse party if they constitute impeaching evidence. Any documents used by a witness while on the stand are subject to inspection to ensure that the whole truth is reflected because of their possible use in court.

Proving Specific Transactions. In proving specific transactions such as purchases and sales of real and personal property, loans, encumbrances, and other commercial events, it is *not* enough for the investigator to obtain the written record of those transactions. Documents and recorded entries, no matter how honestly made, are not in themselves facts. They are written descriptions of events but are not in themselves proof of the events. Consequently, witnesses should be produced who will testify about the transactions and authenticate the documents. During the investigation, parties to the transactions should be questioned to determine whether the documents or entries truthfully relate all the facts and that there are no additional facts or circumstances which have *not* been recorded. The following examples illustrate this principle:

- If the case involves proving sales by the subject of the investigation, the vendees should be interviewed to determine whether checks and invoices represent all the transactions with the subject, whether the documents truthfully record the events, whether additional sums might have been paid or refunded, whether there were any other methods of payment or other parties to the transaction, and whether there is other relevant information.

- A contract of sale, settlement sheet, closing statement, or recorded deed does not necessarily reflect all the facts involved in a real estate transaction. Currently payments over and above those shown in the instrument and nominees or other "straw parties" may be revealed through questioning the parties to the transaction. Mortgages and other encumbrances may not actually exist, although recorded documents seem to evidence such facts. Proof of real estate transactions should therefore include the testimony of the parties involved.

No question of admissibility is involved when different items of documentary evidence may be used to prove a fact. The only thing involved in such a case is the weight of the evidence, which is determined by the jury in the same way as the weight of any other evidence placed before it. Thus, where the government is trying to prove that a third party made purchases from the subject, a cancelled check of the third party to the order of the subject will not be excluded from evidence merely because purchase invoices, purchase journals, or cash disbursements books of the party, although available, have not been produced. The fact that the check itself may not be the best proof of payment for a purchase is a factual question for the jury. However, complete documentation of every transaction should be obtained whenever possible.

Official Records

Statutory Provisions Regarding Official Records.   The admissibility of official (public) records and copies or transcripts thereof in federal proceedings is covered by the provisions of the Federal Rules of Evidence, the United States Code, and the rules of criminal and civil procedure.

Authentication of Official Records.   As a condition precedent to admissibility of documentary evidence, the evidence must be authenticated; that is, it must be established that the item of evidence is what it is supposed to be. For example, it must be shown that a certain document sought to be introduced in evidence actually is an official record of a particular state government. Authentication, however, does not mean that the document necessarily will be admitted in evidence. It may be inadmissible for reasons such as hearsay.

The admissibility of official records and copies or transcripts thereof is provided by the Federal Rules of Evidence. Rule 1005 (Public Records) states that *"the contents of an official record, or of a document authorized to be recorded or filed and actually recorded or filed, including data compilations in any form, if otherwise admissible, may be proven by copy, certified as correct in accordance with Rule 902 or testified to be correct by a witness who has compared it with the original. If a copy which complies with the foregoing cannot be obtained by the exercise of reasonable diligence, then other evidence of the contents may be given. Under this rule, there is no requirement that the original be introduced."*

Rule 902, F.R.E., provides that extrinsic evidence of authenticity as a condition precedent to admissibility is not required for certain types of documents, including public documents under seal, certified copies of public records (mentioned in Rule 1005), newspapers and periodicals, trade inscriptions and the like (e.g., signs, tags or labels purporting to have been affixed in the course of business and indicating ownership, control, or origin), and commercial paper and related documents to the extent provided by general commercial law. As mentioned above, this does not mean that the documents necessarily will be admitted. For example, a newspaper may not be admissible on the ground of irrelevancy.

A method of authentication of copies of federal records is set forth in the Federal Rules of Civil Procedure which is made applicable to criminal cases by Rule 27 of the Federal Rules of Criminal Procedure. Authentication of a copy of a government record under these rules would consist of a certification by the officer having custody of the records and verification of the official status of the certifying officer by a federal district judge over the seal of the court.

State and Territorial Statutes and Proceedings. The admissibility of copies of legislative acts of any state, territory or possession of the United States and of court records and judicial proceedings is provided for in the United States Code as follows (28 U.S.C. 1738): *"Such acts, records and judicial proceedings or copies thereof, so authenticated, shall have the same full faith and credit in every court within the United States and its territories and possessions as they have by law or usage in the courts of such state, territory or possession from which they are taken."*

The procedures for authentication of the above records are recited in the same section of the code.

Nonjudicial records or books kept in any public office of any state, territory or possession of the United States, or copies thereof, are made admissible by the United States Code and given full faith and credit upon proper authentication (28 U.S.C. 1739). Rules 901 and 902, F.R.E., provide more liberal procedures for authentication of the documents covered in this section of the text.

Chain of Custody

Legal Requirements for Chain of Custody. Chain of Custody is a term usually applied to the preservation, by its successive custodians, of the instrument of a crime or any relevant writing in its original condition. Documents or other physical objects may be the instrumentalities used to commit a crime and are generally admissible as such. However, the trial judge must be satisfied that the writing or other physical object is in the same condition as it was when the crime was committed. Consequently, the witness through whom the instrument is sought to be introduced must be able to identify it as being in the same condition as when it was recovered. Investigators must, therefore, promptly identify and preserve in original condition all evidentiary matter that may be offered into evidence.

Identification of Seized Documentary Evidence. In order that a seized document may be admissible as evidence, it is necessary to prove that it is the document that was seized and that it is in the same condition as it was when seized. Since several persons may handle it in the interval between the seizure and the trial of the case, it should be adequately marked at the time of seizure for later identification, and its custody must be shown from that time until it is introduced in court.

An investigator who seizes documents should at once identify them by some marking so that he can later testify that they are the documents seized and that they are in the same condition as they were when seized. He may, for instance, put his initials and the date of seizure on the margin, in a corner or some other inconspicuous place on the front, or on the back of each document. If circumstances indicate that such marking may render the document subject to attack on the ground that it has been defaced or that it is not in the same condition as when seized, the investigator, after making a photostat or other copy for comparison or for use as an exhibit to his report, may put the document into an envelope and write a description and any other identifying information on the face of the envelope and seal the envelope.

Constitutional and Statutory Provisions Relating to Financial Investigations

Constitutional Provisions. The principal constitutional limitations relating to investigative techniques are the fourth, fifth, and sixth amendments to the U.S. Constitution and similar provisions in the state constitution.

The Fourth Amendment provides: *"The right of the people to be secure in their persons, houses, papers and effects, against unreasonable searches and seizures, shall not be violated, and no warrants shall issue, but upon probable cause, supported by oath or affirmation, and particularly describing the place to be searched and the persons or things to be seized."* This protection is given to corporations as well as individuals.

The relevant part of the U.S. Constitution's Fifth Amendment provides: *"No person shall be compelled in any criminal case to be a witness against himself, nor shall he be deprived of life, liberty or property without due process of law."* This privilege is given only to individuals, not to corporations.

The relevant part of the U.S. Constitution's Sixth Amendment states: *"In all criminal prosecutions the accused shall enjoy the right to have the assistance of counsel for his defense."*

Statutory Provisions. Within these constitutional guidelines, statutes can be passed permitting financial investigations. Challenges to financial investigations have been litigated primarily in federal courts, so most of the discussion will deal with federal court decisions based on the federal constitution and statutes.

U.S. Supreme Court decisions based on the U.S. Constitution are binding on state courts and state officers. Federal court decisions relating to federal statutes are not directly binding on state officers, since they operate under state statutes. But most state statutes are similar to the federal statutes; so the rulings on similar provisions are quite relevant to how state courts may interpret their statutes.

Access to Books and Papers. Federal and many state statutes provide that certain auditors can examine a subject's books or papers and summon subjects (including third-party witnesses) to come before them to give testimony or bring records. But – what about the Fourth Amendment prohibition against illegal searches except on probable cause? Isn't it a search when you tell someone you want to look through his records?

And what about the Fifth Amendment privilege against self-incrimination? If you ask him questions about his records, isn't he likely to incriminate himself? Or if you tell him to give you a copy of his records, might not this also incriminate him? Or if you tell him he can't have his lawyer present, doesn't this violate his right to counsel (Sixth Amendment)?

If an investigator goes to a subject and asks to see his books or records or to check his liquor bottles, what are the rights of that person under the Fourth Amendment? If the subject voluntarily consents to let the investigator inspect or copy his records, he has waived his Fourth Amendment constitutional rights. The key word is "voluntarily."

If any trickery or coercion is used by the investigator, the consent isn't voluntary. So if you promise him that if he cooperates he won't be prosecuted, and he subsequently is, – you don't have voluntary consent. Any evidence you get from a search made on that basis may subsequently be suppressed by the courts. This is the *exclusionary rule* – if law enforcement officers get physical evidence, admissions, confessions, or tips which lead to evidence in ways which violate the constitution or statutes, and the victim makes a motion to suppress the evidence, the courts will order it excluded from the trial.

Some courts have permitted certain types of regulatory searches to be made without warrants – but most say you can't search without a warrant without consent, although the standards for finding consent are more loosely enforced in regulatory search cases than in criminal search cases.

If the person doesn't consent, you can do one of two things:

- Get a summons or subpoena, or

- Get a search warrant.

The Summons or Subpoena. In most states certain employees of state government can issue a subpoena requiring witnesses to appear and, if necessary, to bring records and papers. The advantage of a summons is that it is not necessary to establish probable cause about a crime, as with a search warrant.

But if you seek a summons or subpoena of the subject's records from him directly, he can claim his Fifth Amendment privilege against self-incrimination. By getting them in this way you would be getting direct testimonial evidence to convict him. Thus, you may reach a dead end here with regard to the summons to the subject himself.

Therefore, even though you probably do not want to summon the subject's records from him, you may want to summon records relating to his financial transactions from others, including his bank or the company he works for.

Privileged Relationships. The rule supporting privileged communications is based on the legislature's belief that it is necessary to maintain the confidentiality of certain communications. It covers only those communications which are a unique product of the relationship. They must have been made in confidence and not in the presence of third parties, unless the speaker has a privileged relationship with the third party – for example, a man talks to his lawyer in front of his wife. Common law has granted the privilege to the following relationships, among others:

- Husband – Wife

- Attorney – Client

Only the holder of a privilege or someone authorized by him can assert a privilege. The privilege can be waived if he fails to assert it, after having notice and an opportunity to assert it. He also waives it if he discloses a significant part of the communication or if the communication is made in the presence of a third party whose presence is not indispensable to the conversation. The presence of a secretary or an interpreter would not abolish the privilege.

The attorney-client privilege is held by the client – not by the lawyer – and the privilege does not terminate at the client's death. The communication is protected only if its purpose was related to legal consultation. An exception is where the attorney was consulted for the purpose of aiding in the perpetration of a crime or fraud or for giving business advice.

10

Interrogation Techniques

Mastering the art of interrogating perpetrators of financial crimes is difficult to achieve. Few investigators are ever fully satisfied with their level of performance in this vital phase of the investigation of financial crimes. Many investigators think of their best questions or tactical approaches after key interrogations have been concluded.

There are several reasons for a lack of proficiency in interrogation techniques: inadequate planning, a reluctance to actually confront the accused with unpleasant matters, and a tendency to underestimate the mental capabilities of the violator. In the latter instance it should be kept in mind that most of the illegal acts committed by violators are premeditated, may involve complex financial transactions, often require the advice and counsel of accountants and attorneys, and require an overall high level of intelligence. Another highly significant reason for a general lack of expertise in this area is inadequate training. Most law enforcement training efforts in interrogation techniques have been directed toward the perpetrators of or witnesses to violent crimes. Even under the most desirable circumstances, formal training in the area of financial crime interrogation techniques has its limitations. There is simply no substitute for experience. Gaining experience, however, without at least some exposure to formal training has obvious pitfalls.

The purpose of this chapter is to alert investigators to some of the key considerations that should be taken into account *before* initially undertaking the difficult task of interrogating financial crime perpetrators. After giving careful consideration to the key elements in the art of interrogation covered in this chapter, investigators can proceed in a more confident manner to carry out this most difficult phase of financial crime investigations.

Distinctions and Definitions

While emphasis in this chapter is on interrogation rather than interviewing techniques, it is important that investigators understand the distinction between the two. They are defined as follows:

- Interviewing involves questioning individuals in order to elicit information and to obtain documentary and physical evidence relating to crimes committed by *others*.

- Interrogating involves questioning those suspected of having committed crimes as well as the questioning of hostile and/or culpable witnesses in order to obtain evidence of their involvement in crimes.

There is often only a subtle distinction between the two techniques. On occasion an interview will shift to an interrogation, usually when it appears that a witness may be culpable, hostile, or otherwise may be deliberately attempting to withhold information. The reverse may also occur when a subject clearly indicates a desire to cooperate and possibly "turn," thereby furnishing evidence against others.

Planning and Preparation

The importance of proper planning and careful preparation for the interrogation of someone under investigation for the commission of a financial crime cannot be overemphasized. It is sheer folly for even the most experienced investigator to walk into an interrogation room and confront someone without carefully working out an interrogation plan. He can be assured that the subject and his attorney have given careful thought and consideration to the manner in which they are going to approach the interrogation. After all, the stakes are high. The subject's freedom may depend on the outcome.

Some of the key factors that should be taken into account in the planning process are as follows:

Use of an Outline vs. List of Questions. The investigator has three alternatives in preparing to interrogate a subject. He can write verbatim questions, prepare a topic outline or rely solely on his memory with no type of written plan. The latter approach is wholly unwise and is not worthy of further comment.

An attempt to interrogate a subject by relying on a list of previously prepared questions usually results in disaster. An investigator who relies on such a "crutch" usually lacks confidence in his ability to think clearly and formulate questions that are logical and pertinent. Continuous use of a list of questions merely compounds the investigator's problems until he reaches a point where he cannot effectively conduct an interrogation. He becomes so intent on following his list of questions he fails to concentrate on the answers of the subject which, after all, is the primary goal of the interrogation process. As a result he seldom if ever develops expertise in formulating "follow up" questions when a reply indicates such a need. Instead, he proceeds methodically, asking questions from the previously prepared list, and rarely achieves his objectives.

Those who prepare sample lists of questions and advocate their use in interrogation courses have seldom had actual interrogation experience or have failed to achieve an acceptable level of success in interrogation. Many interrogation instructors appear to be writers rather than interrogators. They seem to enjoy developing unrealistic scenarios, often laced with subtle, simplistic humor.

Interrogation training is not funny, nor should it be designed to entertain students. It is a difficult subject to teach as well as a most challenging technique to learn. There is simply no room for actors or humorists in the development of the training materials.

The use of a topic outline, on the other hand, offers many advantages. Subject matter can be listed briefly in what appears, during preparation, to be logical order. It can easily be rearranged during an actual interrogation by lining out the topic and re-inserting it in another place in the outline *without* disrupting the interrogator's concentration on the subject's answers. Appropriate "follow-up" questions can more readily be asked when the interrogator has only to keep in mind a category rather than a list of questions. It is then easy to avoid the pitfall of blindly following a list of questions in sequential order when a subject's answer to the preceding question causes the next question on the list to be irrelevant or even silly. The use of a topic outline also ensures that an investigator will formulate his own questions rather than copy lists of questions from old training materials and attempt to tailor or force someone else's questions to meet the needs of a particular interrogation.

Use of a topic outline need not necessarily be followed throughout an interrogation. Some degree of flexibility is desirable. Occasionally a *highly* technical question may need to be written out if careful wording of the question is needed to convey complete understanding. In those instances the questions should be written in the topic outline and actually read out loud.

An opening statement at the outset of an interrogation may also be written in advance to ensure that the subject clearly understands *why* he has been asked to appear and answer questions. This approach cuts off an often-used defense that the subject didn't understand why he had been asked to appear as a witness and didn't know that he was under investigation. Informing a subject of his constitutional rights should always be written in the topic outline to ensure that there is no misunderstanding on the part of the subject as to his right to refuse to answer questions.

Both of the above techniques are covered in greater detail in subsequent sections of this chapter. They are mentioned here only to illustrate the need for flexibility in the use of a topic outline.

Timing. Another key factor that should be given careful consideration in the interrogation planning process is the timing of an interrogation. There are advantages and disadvantages to questioning a subject at the outset, during the course of, or at the conclusion of an investigation. The decision as to when to question the subject should be made on a case-by-case basis.

One of the advantages of an interrogation early in an investigation, particularly in those cases where the subject is cooperative, is that it can save a considerable amount of time and effort in making third-party inquiries. Another advantage is that pertinent documents are usually more readily available. In addition, facts and circumstances related to the subject's questionable conduct are fresh in his or her mind and it is more difficult to claim a loss of memory.

Observing the subject's attitude, demeanor, and reaction to questions may also provide "indicators" as to whether or not the subject has, in fact, committed a crime. These observations, together with other information already obtained, may be helpful to an investigator in determining whether or not to proceed further with an investigation that may have questionable prosecution potential.

On the other hand, there are pitfalls in conducting an early interrogation. It not only discloses to the subject the fact that he is under criminal investigation but the very nature of the investigator's questions may disclose the extent of the investigator's knowledge of the violation and the overall direction that the investigation is taking. Armed with this information the subject may attempt to destroy or alter documentary evidence or adversely influence the testimony of potential witnesses.

One of the factors in favor of an interrogation of a subject at the conclusion of an investigation is that it enables an investigator to confront a subject with the evidence that has been gathered against him or her. Many investigators develop a particular talent in the use of a confrontation technique and as a result are able to obtain full confessions or at least partial admissions of guilt.

All of the above factors should be carefully considered during the planning phase and *before* a decision is made to interrogate.

A general rule that may be helpful in making decisions as to the timing of interrogations is that friendly witnesses should be questioned first, *before* hostile witnesses and/or subjects. Following this general rule enables an investigator to proceed with the interrogation of the latter armed with as much background information as possible. In addition any later attempts by the subject to influence the testimony of witnesses will be impeded.

Selection of Location.   There are several factors that should be considered before deciding where a subject should be iinterrogated. A decision should be made on a case-by-case basis taking the following factors into account.

There are several advantages to conducting an interrogation at an investigator's office. The investigator's files are more readily available if needed. Interruptions can be controlled. Stenographers or recording facilities are readily available. (Recording of testimony is discussed in depth in a subsequent section of this chapter.) While the effectiveness and advisability of the use of so-called psychological techniques during an interrogation are questionable, there is some merit to removing a subject from familiar surroundings to an unfamiliar and less relaxed atmosphere.

On the other hand, if an interrogation is conducted at the subject's home or office, records are in all probability available. This makes it more difficult for him or her to refuse to make the records available for examination. It also makes it more difficult to claim a loss of memory when answering key questions since the records are at hand from which to refresh recollection.

The subject's home or office is also the best alternative in those instances when an investigator seeks to catch him or her off guard. If no prior appointment is made an investigator may elect to merely drop by the office or home, the advantage being that the subject will not have had time to prepare for an interrogation. There is the added advantage of not having the subject's attorney present. In that situation, however, it is imperative that the subject be informed of his constitutional rights.

Recording Alternatives

Regardless of the manner in which testimony of a subject is obtained, an investigator should *always* assume that *everything* is being recorded, either overtly by the investigator (with permission of all parties) or covertly by a subject or his representative. If an investigator automatically makes this assumption and keeps it in mind during the course of *every* contact with a subject, there is far less danger of controversy or embarrassment over what was said or implied during the course of conversations.

Accordingly, all subsequent discussion in this chapter on interrogation strategies is based on the assumption that *all* conversations with a subject, formal or informal, are being recorded in some manner by one of the parties. This is a highly realistic assumption when the advanced state of the art of miniature recording equipment is taken into account.

Verbatim Recordings. The best way to obtain the testimony of a subject is to have a stenographic reporter present during an interrogation. He or she should take shorthand notes or utilize a stenotype machine to record the *entire* proceeding. A verbatim transcript of the entire proceeding should be prepared from the notes or stenotype as soon as possible by the same recorder. It is recognized, however, that the high cost of skilled stenographic services and the lack of availability of most stenographic personnel in this highly special-ized field makes the use of this technique unattainable by most investigative agencies and businesses.

The best alternative to the use of a stenographic reporter is the use of a tape recorder. In some respects this is even superior to the use of a stenographer since no one can legitimately question the accuracy of the recording, thereby assuring both parties to the interrogation of an accurate record.

In the event that a tape recorder is used, the following guidelines should be considered:

- In order to ensure optimum recording quality the best available recording equipment should be used.

- To avoid unnecessary interruptions the slowest recording speed and longest tapes should be used.

- The tape recorder should be placed on a separate table, if possible, in order that its presence doesn't create unnecessary distraction.

- If possible, microphones (miniaturized, on stands) should be placed at each end of the interrogation table for use by the interrogator and the subject. If available, a high quality microphone should be placed on the same table as the recorder.

The tape recorder should be turned on as soon as all parties to the interrogation are present.

The investigator should *not* ask the subject for permission to record the interrogation. He should take a positive approach, stating that he plans to record the proceeding in order that there will be no misunderstanding as to what each party has stated, thereby guaranteeing an accurate record. If the subject then indicates a reluctance to the use of the recorder, the investigator should ask *why* he or she objects. In most instances, the "why" will result in agreement to the recording of the proceedings, since it is difficult for anyone to offer a logical reason for refusing to permit an accurate record to be made. The investigator should proceed with a short introductory statement for the record, identifying the parties who are present, stating the date, location, time of day, and the fact that all parties agree to the recording of the proceedings.

Affidavits – Written Statements. The next best alternative to the use of a tape-recorded question and answer interrogation is an affidavit. It can only be used, however, if the investigator has authority to administer an oath. In the event that an investigator does not have the authority to administer an oath, a written statement signed by the subject is the next best alternative. The only distinction between the two alternatives is that the former is sworn to by the subject. In both instances, the following precautions should be taken:

The statement should be made using a format approved by appropriate counsel of the investigator's agency or the local prosecutor who will ultimately consider the case for prosecution. No illustration of a proposed format is contained in this text since it may be in conflict with the format utilized in the investigator's jurisdiction.

Regardless of format, and unless there are overriding circumstances, the statement should be in the handwriting of the subject or dictated by him to a stenographer or recording device. This ensures that the statement reflects the subject's testimony rather than the testimony of the investigator.

When the statement is prepared it should be reviewed by all parties for possible errors. Any changes that result must be initialed by the subject. If the statement consists of more than one page, each page should be initialed by the subject on the lower right-hand corner. A diagonal line should be drawn on the last page from the last line of the statement to the signature line to ensure that nothing can be added to the statement improperly. No copies of the statement should be made or offered to the subject unless he specifically requests one.

Memorandums of Interviews – Notes. If a subject refuses to permit the recording of his testimony and also refuses to sign an affidavit or unsworn statement, the investigator should prepare a comprehensive memorandum of his conversation with the subject as soon as possible.

The investigator should make notations during the course of the interrogation to assist him in preparing the memorandum. The extent to which an investigator can successfully take notes during the course of an interrogation without jeopardizing his ability to concentrate on the subject's testimony will vary. Some investigators develop considerable note taking skills, some even take shorthand courses to sharpen their skills.

The more effective an investigator becomes in taking comprehensive notes the more credible his memorandums of conversations are from an evidentiary standpoint. In any event *all* notes made by the investigator of his conversations with a subject, whether they are used in the preparation of memorandums of conversations or not, should be carefully preserved in the event that they are ultimately needed by a prosecutor. The latter may wish to review an investigator's notes to satisfy himself as to the overall credibility of an investigator's memorandums of interview. He may need to make copies available to the defendant upon order of the Court during argument of pretrial motions, or he may find them useful during a trial in cross-examining the defendant or possibly in re-direct examination of an investigator.

As stated earlier in this chapter relative to the format of affidavits, investigators should check with counsel of their agencies or business entities or with their local prosecutors to determine their preferences as to the format of memorandums of interviews.

❯ *Interrogation Techniques* ❮

The following guidelines are, as indicated earlier in this chapter, based on the assumption that *all* interrogations are being recorded by one of the parties. Therefore, in order that the record clearly reflects the proceedings and in order to demonstrate that the investigator is in control of all aspects of the proceedings, a logical order of procedure from the outset of the interrogation should be followed. A suggested sequence of events is as follows:

Introductory Statement. When all parties arrive in the interrogation room the investigator should introduce himself and, as stated earlier in the chapter, inform the subject that he plans to record the proceedings in order to ensure that an accurate record can be obtained. After turning on the recorder the investigator should make a short introductory statement identifying all of the parties who are present, stating the date, time of day, location, and that all parties have agreed to the recording of the proceedings.

The next step in the introductory process is of considerable importance. The investigator should inform the subject *why* he has been asked to appear and answer questions.

If the nature of the violation under investigation is somewhat complex, and since it is vitally important that the subject fully understand why he has been asked to appear for questioning, it may be necessary for the investigator to read this information from a previously prepared written statement inserted into his topic outline. A suggested format is as follows:

> *"Mr.___________, you have been asked to appear today to answer questions concerning your alleged violation of the ________ laws of the State of ____________."*

Administering Oath. Following the introductory statement the investigator should administer an oath, if he has such power. The investigator should administer the oath by asking the subject to stand and raise his right hand.

Again, an investigator may prefer to read a prepared statement from his topic outline. A suggested format is as follows:

> *"Mr. _____________, do you swear that your answers to the questions to be asked during these proceedings today will be the truth, the whole truth and nothing but the truth, so help you God?"*

If the subject objects to the wording of the oath on religious grounds, the last phrase of the oath should be eliminated. The term "swear," if offensive to the subject, may be changed to "affirm." The subject should then be advised that he may sit down.

If the subject refuses to testify under oath he should be asked the "key" question, Why? In many instances he or she will then agree to taking an oath, as it is most difficult if not impossible to offer a logical explanation for refusing to give sworn testimony. It also becomes apparent to most people that to refuse to testify under oath may create an inference that they intend to lie.

In any event, if the subject persists in his refusal, and unless it violates policy of the agency, the investigator should proceed with the interrogation on the premise that unsworn testimony is better than no testimony.

Constitutional Rights. The next step, if appropriate, is to inform the subject of his constitutional rights. As indicated earlier in the chapter, the information should be written verbatim into the topic outline to ensure that no pertinent language is overlooked. It is strongly recommended that the language used to inform the subject of his constitutional rights and the manner in which it is administered be cleared with the local prosecutor, the state attorney general, the local U.S. Attorney, or the appropriate agency legal counsel, in order to ensure that it conforms with local, state, or federal policy, custom, and/or procedure. For this reason a suggested format is not included in this text even though any variance with a format required by the investigator's agency may be minor. The consequence of error is too important.

The investigator should make sure that he obtains a positive response from the subject that he understands his rights. He should be asked the following direct concise question: *"Do you understand your constitutional rights as I have just stated them, Mr. _______?"* If his reply is not clearly affirmative, clarification should be made immediately before proceeding.

If the subject clearly states that he understands his rights, don't ask him if he is then ready to proceed; just go ahead and question him. Asking a follow-up question such as *"Are you now willing to continue?"* may suggest to him that he can change his mind.

In furnishing information to a subject concerning his constitutional rights, avoid the use of the words "warn" or "advise." You are *not* warning a subject, nor are you *advising* him. You are *informing* him. The latter is your responsibility. The subject obtains *advice* from his attorney. The term, "warn" implies a threat, may cause unnecessary concern on the part of the subject and may enable him to, at the time of trial, disavow his testimony by claiming he was frightened by the "warning" and became confused.

If a subject refuses to answer questions by invoking his Fifth Amendment rights, ask him why he is refusing. Remind him that he can only refuse to answer questions if he feels that his answers would incriminate *him*, not someone else.

Perhaps the most important point to remember concerning the manner in which a criminal investigator informs a subject of his constitutional rights is to never, in any way or manner, attempt to be devious, misleading, or vague. It can only result in embarrassment to the agency and, ultimately, to the criminal investigator and the prosecutor. It may also result in the Court's refusing to admit into evidence any of the admissions made.

Personal History. After all of the preliminary matters have been taken care of the subject should be asked a series of questions concerning his personal history: his full name, address, date and place of birth, education, marital status, dependents, employment record, and any other similar matters that may be pertinent. Questions of this nature tend to relax both the subject and the investigator, aid in establishing rapport, and prepare the investigator to ask questions concerning the alleged violation.

In obtaining the above personal history, investigators should never ask a subject questions concerning any prior criminal record. Inserting this type of information may render the transcript of the proceedings inadmissible during a forthcoming trial since the trial judge may rule that references to a prior criminal record may be prejudicial.

General vs. Specific Questions.   After the personal history has been obtained, get to the heart of the matter in question. As a rule, start with a general question. For example, ask

> *"Tell me what you know about the ABC Company contract with*
> *XYZ County."*

Then follow up with specific questions as necessary. By using this technique you can determine what the subject knows *before* indicating by your specific questions what you already know or don't know about the matter in question.

Try to encourage a subject to disclose his knowledge about a particular matter by the manner in which your questions are formulated. For example, ask a target the following:

> *"I understand that you were present when Mr. __________ signed*
> *the contract with ABC Company. Would you describe what*
> *happened on that occasion?"*

> Rather than:

> *"Were you present when, etc.............."*

Books and Records.   If books and records are pertinent to the investigation, be sure and obtain the following information:

- A description of each pertinent record (i.e., journal, ledger, check stubs, diary, minute book, etc.).

- Identity of individuals who maintained each record and the period of time that they maintained them.

- The degree of responsibility, if any, of the subject in maintaining or reviewing them.

- The present location of the records.

- Whether or not the subject is willing to submit them to the investigator for examination.

Identification of Documents.   In most financial crime investigations it is often necessary for a subject to identify one or more documents involved in the alleged crime. It is important to remember that *each* document should be identified *individually*, particularly those documents that have a direct relationship to the crime. For example in a false travel voucher case, each travel voucher should be identified by asking a question similar to the following:

> *"Mr. _______________, I have handed you what appears to be your travel voucher that you submitted to the XYZ Company for the month of January, 19___ and ask you if the signature that appears in the lower left-hand corner of the front of the voucher is your signature?"*

The same technique *must* be employed for all documents pertinent to proving the fraud. A blanket endorsement by the subject is not satisfactory. The questions of the investigator must ensure that *each* document and signature, if pertinent, are clearly identified.

Don't interrupt the subject when he is answering a question. Even if he strays from the subject, let him wander within reasonable limitations. You may pick up additional pertinent information.

Hostile questions many times will lead to a premature termination of an interrogation. Therefore, don't ask hostile questions until all of the seemingly innocuous questions have been asked and answered.

Don't ask compound questions. Make sure that each question requires only one answer.

Give the subject ample time to answer questions. If, however, he appears to be unable or unwilling to answer a question be sure that the record reflects his reluctance. In those circumstances the following statement by the investigator may be appropriate:

> *"Mr. _______________, three minutes have passed since I asked you whether or not you.........Why haven't you answered the question?"*

Be sure that you understand the subject's answers. If, for some reason, his answer is not clear, tell him that you don't understand his answer and ask him to clarify it.

Be sure that you obtain all pertinent facts about each topic in question. Don't abandon the topic when you think you have enough because of a fear that the subject may say something that is harmful to the investigation. It is far better to get *all* of the facts during the course of the investigation than have the prosecutor obtain adverse information for the first time during the course of a trial.

When appropriate, confront the subject with the fact that he has lied. Ask him *why* he lied. Study his reaction to confrontation; i.e., nervousness, dry mouth, sweating, pulsing carotid artery, twitching, shortness of breath, etc.

Don't accept general answers or statements that fail to pinpoint responsibility for specific acts. Use the "who, when, where, how, and why" technique to its fullest extent.

Don't be fooled by attempts to gain your sympathy. Be objective and pleasant, but also be firm.

Discourage the subject from asking questions. Keep in mind that the purpose of the proceeding is for the *subject* to answer questions, *not* the investigator. When the subject asks a question, answer his question with a question. For example, the investigator may respond as follows:

"Why do you ask that, Mr. _________?"

or

"Why does that concern you, Mr. _________?"

or

"What brought that question to your mind, Mr. _________?"

Don't refer to the subject or his attorney by their first names or show any undue familiarity. Discourage them from addressing you by your first name if possible. In the event that the transcript is read aloud during the course of a trial, it creates an impression to the jury that perhaps the matter under investigation wasn't very serious.

Control all aspects of the interrogation. Maintain order. Control the tempo of the questions and answers. Make sure that only one person is speaking at a time in order that the recording is intelligible.

Unless it appears to be helpful, discourage the subject's attorney from asking questions. If necessary remind him that he is present only to advise his client whether or not to answer questions. On the other hand, however, keep in mind that any statements made by the attorney in the presence of the subject are admissible against the subject unless he clearly disavows them.

Don't underestimate the ability of the subject. Keep in mind he has allegedly committed a financial crime. He has demonstrated an ability to make money. His crime was probably premeditated and was possibly carried out with the advice, guidance, and counsel of an accountant and/or an attorney.

Resist requests by the subject or his attorney for "off the record" discussions if the interrogation is being recorded. Point out the many advantages to both parties of having an accurate and complete record. If it cannot be avoided (without terminating the proceeding prematurely), try to summarize what was said *on the record* at the conclusion of the off-record discussion. If the target is unwilling to permit the summary to be included in the record, then make notes of the substance of the off-record discussion and attach the notes to the transcript of the proceeding.

Encourage the subject to talk freely. However, balance this advantage with the disadvantage of permitting him to wander endlessly into irrelevant matters.

Listen carefully to all answers. If an answer is incomplete or ambiguous, follow up with appropriate questions. If an answer suggests a new avenue of inquiry, follow up right away, or make a note to remind yourself to develop the new lead later in the interrogation.

Keep in mind that you may not get a second chance to interrogate a subject. Always make that assumption, and plan your strategy accordingly.

If the subject's answers appear to show a pattern of evasiveness, increase the degree of firmness and, again, follow up with probing questions.

Don't ask leading questions that require a yes or no answer unless there appears to be no alternative. The subject is testifying, not the investigator. Ask short, concise, succinct questions that are relatively easy to understand, and let the subject answer them.

Regardless of the nature of the alleged violation, *always* ask the subject if he has a safe deposit box, what he keeps in the box, and whether or not he will permit you to (in his presence) inventory its contents immediately following the conclusion of the interrogation.

Inform the subject that any entrance into the box by him subsequent to the interrogation and *before* the time of the joint inventory creates an inference that he may have removed items from the box that may be incriminating. If the subject refuses the investigator's request to inventory the box he should, again, be asked the most important question in an interrogation proceeding, Why?

Again, regardless of the nature of the alleged violation, always ask the subject if he has a checking account, if he keeps his cancelled checks, if so, for how long a period, and whether or not you can examine them. Cancelled checks are a tremendous source of leads in making an expenditure analysis in identifying the source of funds that may be pertinent to the receipt or payment of bribes, pay-offs, etc., and to the identification of associates. If the subject refuses to turn over his cancelled checks for examination he, again, should be asked, Why?

When all of the areas of interest contained in the investigator's topic outline have been thoroughly covered, the investigator should take the following precautions in closing the interrogation:

- Leave the door open for further questioning. Ask the subject if he is willing to answer further questions if the need should arise. Don't state or even infer that he will not be questioned again.

- Ask the subject if all of his answers were made freely and voluntarily, without promise of reward, and free of threats.

- Don't offer the subject a copy of the transcript of the proceedings. Resist any request for a copy by stating that it will be furnished if and/or when a transcript is made.

- Don't thank the subject for his cooperation. Merely state that you have "no further questions at this time."

Finally, every investigator should develop his own checklist of general admonitions and should review them frequently. Some of the key admonitions that should be included on the checklist are as follows.

1. Subdue all prejudices.

2. Keep an open mind.

3. Don't offer compromises or make misleading statements.

4. Don't get mad or sarcastic.

5. Don't ask the subject's attorney if he wants to ask any questions.

6. If appropriate, ask the subject *why* he committed the alleged crime. Who knows, he may tell you.

7. Don't let the subject or his attorney see your outline or notes.

8. Don't ridicule or belittle the subject.

9. Don't consider success a victory. Conceal your emotions.

10. Avoid political or religious matters.

11. Avoid showing signs of nervousness.

12. Avoid questions that may unnecessarily antagonize the subject.

13. Be dominant without being domineering.

14. Display confidence in your course of action. Show that you are in control.

15. Be a patient listener.

Keep in mind the following most important questions:

- *Why?*

- *Why not?*

- *How do you know?*

11

Internal Banking Procedures

Examining cancelled checks and related financial data often require an ability to interpret processing codes placed on documents by financial institutions. In addition, it is often helpful to know the record retention requirements imposed by the federal government on financial institutions. Pertinent information covering these areas is included in this chapter.

Identifying Cashed Checks

All banks use a series of codes or symbols to indicate on a check the nature of its disposition. Of particular interest to an investigator are those checks received from others that have been cashed by a subject as well as checks drawn on a subject's checking account that have been cashed by the subject. In both instances, the subject's actions are indicators of an attempt to destroy an audit trail of his financial transactions by converting funds to currency before making expenditures.

The following illustration shows the "cashed" code used by one of the major banks in the Mid-Atlantic states. It is one of the most commonly used codes and is stamped on the face of cashed checks.

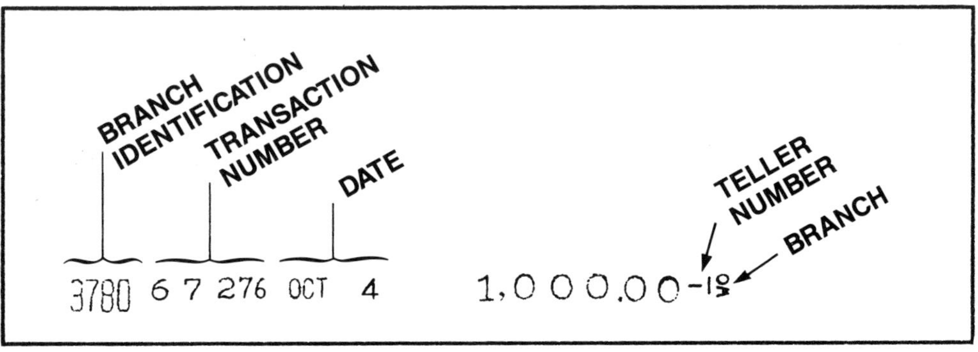

Examples of "cashed" codes used by banks in Western states are illustrated below: (In each instance the codes are stamped on the face of checks.)

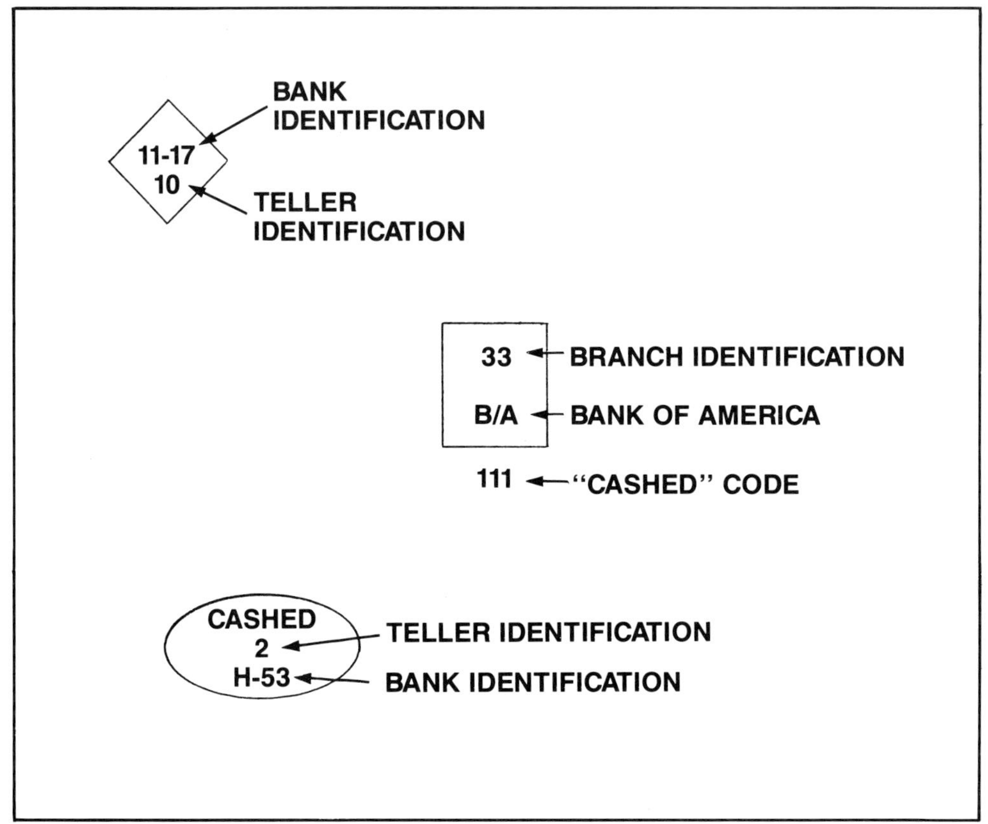

Investigators should contact appropriate officials of principal banks within their geographic area of investigative jurisdiction to determine the specific codes used to indicate the manner in which checks are negotiated. Their inquiries should not be limited to the "cashed" codes. They should include the identification of bank codes used to identify the disposition of *all* checks accepted by banks from its customers for payment, whether they are drawn on the bank where the checks are being negotiated or drawn on other banks. Investigators will then be able to read the codes and be able to more readily determine the nature of specific transactions, i.e., cashed checks, checks deposited to checking or savings accounts, checks used to make loan payments, purchase cashier's checks travelers' checks, etc.

○ *Identifying New Accounts* ○

Beginning in 1990 many states adopted a new encoding requirement on all depositors' printed checks. In either the left upper corner, adjacent to the account holder's name, or in the right upper corner, left of the ABA Transit Number, the month and year that the account was opened is imprinted. One of the purposes of the new requirement is to alert merchants to the possibility that a customer may be issuing a check on a newly opened account with insufficient funds on deposit to cover the check. The value of the information to an investigator is that he or she can readily determine when a checking account has been opened without obtaining a copy of the signature card or initial monthly statement.

○ *American Bankers' Association (ABA)* ○ *Bank Identification Codes*

All checks printed for use by banks and their customers in the United States contain a series of numbers in the upper right hand corner on the face of the checks. These numbers represent an identification code developed by the American Bankers' Association and are usually referred to as the "ABA Transit Number." The code is illustrated below:

The following illustration shows how the ABA Transit Number Identification Code can be interpreted so that individual banks can be identified:

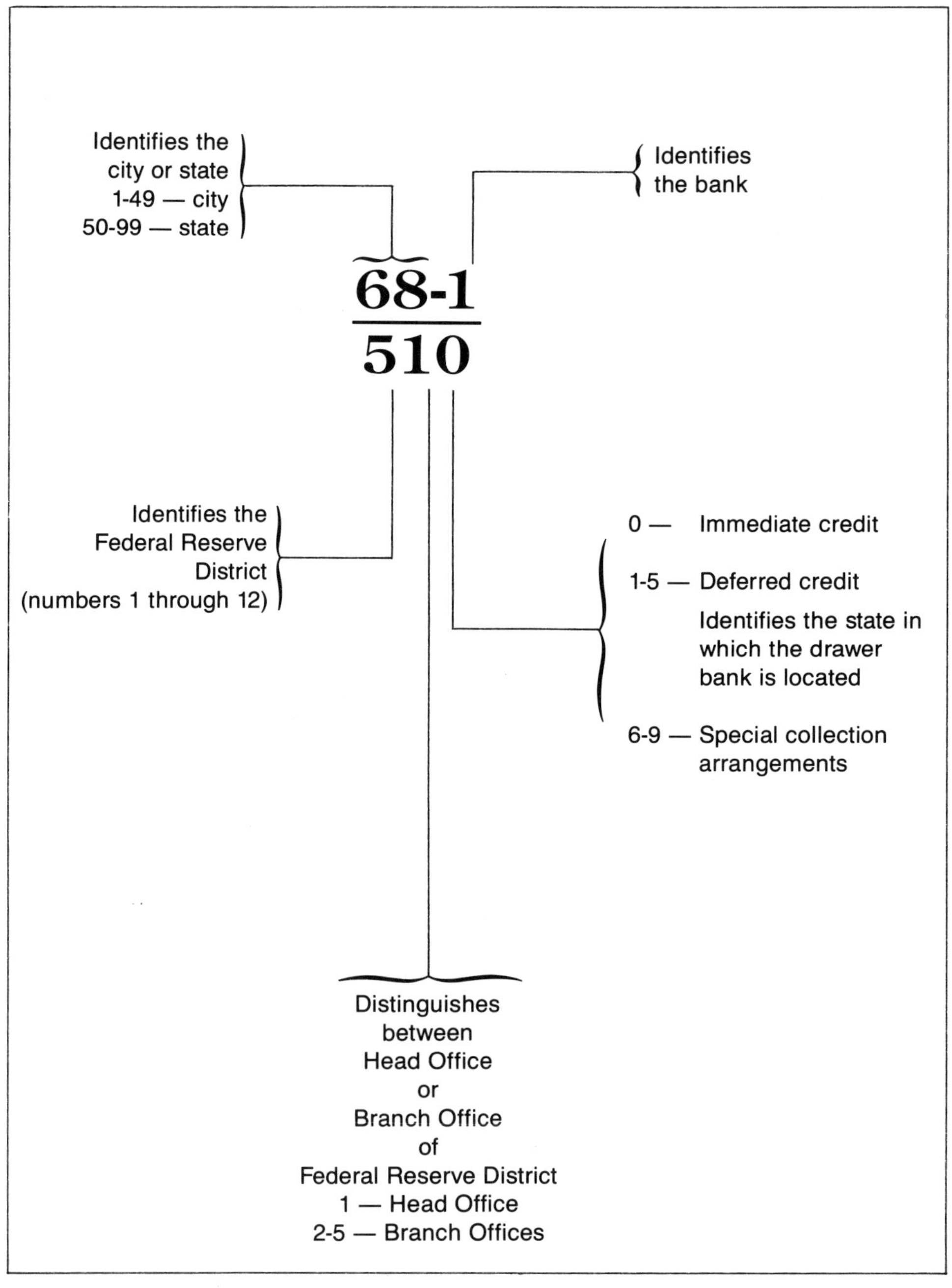

A complete listing of the ABA Numerical System Identification Code is as follows:

Index to Prefix Numbers of Cities and States

Numbers 1 thru 49 inclusive are Prefixes for Cities.
Numbers 50 thru 99 inclusive are Prefixes for States.
Prefix Numbers 50 thru 58 are Eastern States.
Prefix Numbers 60 thru 69 are Southeastern States.
Prefix Numbers 70 thru 79 are Central States.

Prefix Numbers 80 thru 88 are Southwestern States.
Prefix Number 89 is Alaska.
Prefix Numbers 90 thru 99 are Western States.
Prefix Number 101 is American Samoa, Caroline Islands, Guam, Mariana Islands, Marshall Islands, Midway Island, Puerto Rico and Virgin Islands

Prefix Numbers of Cities in Numerical Order

1 New York, N.Y.
2 Chicago, Ill.
3 Philadelphia, Pa.
4 St. Louis, Mo.
5 Boston, Mass.
6 Cleveland, Ohio
7 Baltimore, Md.
8 Pittsburgh, Pa.
9 Detroit, Mich.
10 Buffalo, N.Y.
11 San Francisco, Calif.
12 Milwaukee, Wis.
13 Cincinnati, Ohio
14 New Orleans, La.
15 Washington, D.C.
16 Los Angeles, Calif.
17 Minneapolis, Minn.

18 Kansas City, Kan.
18 Kansas City, Mo.
19 Seattle, Wash.
20 Indianapolis, Ind.
21 Louisville, Ky.
22 St. Paul, Minn.
23 Denver, Colo.
24 Portland, Ore.
25 Columbus, Ohio
26 Memphis, Tenn.
27 Omaha, Neb.
28 Spokane, Wash.
29 Albany, N.Y.
30 San Antonio, Texas
31 Salt Lake City, Utah
32 Dallas, Texas
33 Des Moines, Iowa

34 Tacoma, Wash.
35 Houston, Texas
36 St. Joseph, Mo.
37 Fort Worth, Texas
38 Savannah, Ga.
39 Oklahoma City, Okla.
40 Wichita, Kan.
41 Sioux City, Iowa
42 Pueblo, Colo.
43 Lincoln, Neb.
44 Topeka, Kan.
45 Dubuque, Iowa
46 Galveston, Texas
47 Cedar Rapids, Iowa
48 Waco, Texas
49 Muskogee, Okla.

Prefix Numbers of Cities in Alphabetical Order

Albany, N.Y.	29
Baltimore, Md.	7
Boston, Mass.	5
Buffalo, N.Y.	10
Cedar Rapids, Iowa	47
Chicago, Ill.	2
Cincinnati, Ohio	13
Cleveland, Ohio	6
Columbus, Ohio	25
Dallas, Texas	32
Denver, Colo.	23
Des Moines, Iowa	33
Detroit, Mich.	9
Dubuque, Iowa	45
Fort Worth, Texas	37
Galveston, Texas	46
Houston, Texas	35
Indianapolis, Ind.	20
Kansas City, Kan.	18
Kansas City, Mo.	18
Lincoln, Neb.	43
Los Angeles, Calif.	16
Louisville, Ky.	21
Memphis, Tenn.	26
Milwaukee, Wis.	12
Minneapolis, Minn.	17
Muskogee, Okla.	49
New Orleans, La.	14
New York, N.Y.	1
Oklahoma City, Okla.	39
Omaha, Neb.	27
Philadelphia, Pa.	3
Pittsburgh, Pa.	8
Portland, Ore.	24
Pueblo, Colo.	42
St. Joseph, Mo.	36
St. Louis, Mo.	4
St. Paul, Minn.	22
Salt Lake City, Utah	31
San Antonio, Texas	30
San Francisco, Calif.	11
Savannah, Ga.	38
Seattle, Wash.	19
Sioux City, Iowa	41
Spokane, Wash.	28
Tacoma, Wash.	34
Topeka, Kan.	44
Waco, Texas	48
Washington, D.C.	15
Wichita, Kan.	40

Prefix Numbers of States, Territories and Dependencies in Numerical Order

50 New York
51 Connecticut
52 Maine
53 Massachusetts
54 New Hampshire
55 New Jersey
56 Ohio
57 Rhode Island
58 Vermont
59 Hawaii
60 Pennsylvania
61 Alabama
62 Delaware
63 Florida
64 Georgia
65 Maryland
66 North Carolina
67 South Carolina
68 Virginia

69 West Virginia
70 Illinois
71 Indiana
72 Iowa
73 Kentucky
74 Michigan
75 Minnesota
76 Nebraska
77 North Dakota
78 South Dakota
79 Wisconsin
80 Missouri
81 Arkansas
82 Colorado
83 Kansas
84 Louisiana
85 Mississippi
86 Oklahoma
87 Tennessee

88 Texas
89 Alaska
90 California
91 Arizona
92 Idaho
93 Montana
94 Nevada
95 New Mexico
96 Oregon
97 Utah
98 Washington
99 Wyoming
101 American Samoa, Guam, Caroline Islands, Mariana Islands, Marshall Islands, Midway Island, Puerto Rico and Virgin Islands

Prefix Numbers of States, Territories and Dependencies in Alphabetical Order

Alabama	61	Louisiana	84	Ohio	56
Alaska	89	Maine	52	Oklahoma	86
American Samoa	101	Mariana Islands	101	Oregon	96
Arizona	91	Marshall Islands	101	Pennsylvania	60
Arkansas	81	Maryland	65	Puerto Rico	101
California	90	Massachusetts	53	Rhode Island	57
Caroline Islands	101	Michigan	74	South Carolina	67
Colorado	82	Midway Island	101	South Dakota	78
Connecticut	51	Minnesota	75	Tennessee	87
Delaware	62	Mississippi	85	Texas	88
Florida	63	Missouri	80	Utah	97
Georgia	64	Montana	93	Vermont	58
Guam	101	Nebraska	76	Virginia	68
Hawaii	59	Nevada	94	Virgin Islands	101
Idaho	92	New Hampshire	54	Washington	98
Illinois	70	New Jersey	55	West Virginia	69
Indiana	71	New Mexico	95	Wisconsin	79
Iowa	72	New York	50	Wyoming	99
Kansas	83	North Carolina	66		
Kentucky	73	North Dakota	77		

L

The identification code of the Federal Reserve Banks that service individual banking institutions is contained in the following illustration (Federal Reserve Bank Routing Symbols shown in italics):

FEDERAL RESERVE BANKS AND BRANCHES

1. Federal Reserve Bank of Boston Head Office	5 - 1 *110*	Little Rock Branch	81 - 13 *820*
2. Federal Reserve Bank of New York Head Office	1 - 120 *210*	Louisville Branch	21 - 59 *830*
Buffalo Branch	10 - 26 *220*	Memphis Branch	26 - 3 *840*
3. Federal Reserve Bank of Philadelphia Head Office	3 - 4 *310*	9. Federal Reserve Bank of Minneapolis Head Office	17 - 8 *910*
		Helena Branch	93 - 26 *920*
4. Federal Reserve Bank of Cleveland Head Office	0 - 1 *410*	10. Federal Reserve Bank of Kansas City Head Office	18 - 4 *1010*
Cincinnati Branch	13 - 43 *420*	Denver Branch	23 - 19 *1020*
Pittsburgh Branch	8 - 30 *430*	Oklahoma City Branch	39 -24 *1030*
5. Federal Reserve Bank of Richmond Head Office	68 - 3 *510*	Omaha Branch	27 -12 *1040*
Baltimore Branch	7 - 27 *520*	11. Federal Reserve Bank of Dallas Head Office	32 - 3 *1110*
Charlotte Branch	66 - 20 *530*	El Paso Branch	88 - 1 *1120*
6. Federal Reserve Bank of Atlanta Head Offic	64 - 14 *610*	Houston Branch	35 - 4 *1130*
Birmingham Branch	61 - 19 *620*	San Antonio Branch	30 - 72 *1140*
Jacksonville Branch	63 - 19 *630*	12. Federal Reserve Bank of San Francisco Head Office	11 - 37 *1210*
Nashville Branch	87 -10 *640*	Los Angeles Branch	16 - 16 *1220*
New Orleans Branch	14 - 21 *650*	Portland Branch	24 - 1 *1230*
7. Federal Reserve Bank of Chicago Head Office	2 - 30 *710*	Salt Lake City Branch	31 - 31 *1240*
Detroit Branch	9 - 29 *720*	Seattle Branch	19 - 1 *1250*
8. Federal Reserve Bank of St. Louis Head Office	4 - 4 *810*		

Bank Record Retention Requirements

The United States Department of the Treasury issued regulations to implement Titles I and II of Public Law 91-508, the Financial Recordkeeping and Currency and Foreign Transactions Reporting Act of 1970. The regulations became effective on July 1, 1972.

The regulations provide that an original, microfilm, or other copy or reproduction of most demand deposits (checking accounts) and savings account records *must* be retained for five years. The records must include:

1. Signature cards;

2. Statements, ledger cards, or other records disclosing all transactions, i.e., deposits and withdrawals; and,

3. Copies of customers' checks, bank drafts, money orders, and cashier's checks drawn on the bank or issued and payable by it.

In addition, banks must retain for a two-year period all records necessary to:

1. Reconstruct a customer's checking account (the records *must* include copies of customer's deposit tickets); and,

2. Trace and supply a description of a check deposited to a customer's checking account.

All of the above requirements apply *only* to checks written or deposits made in excess of $100.00. It should be noted, however, that most banks find that it is cheaper to microfilm *all* pertinent records, including those checks and deposits in amounts of *less* than $100.00, rather than sort their records into two categories. Therefore, if a particular transaction of less than $100.00 appears to be of particular interest to an investigator, there is a strong likelihood that the necessary records are available to identify the transaction.

The regulations further provide that whatever system banks use to photocopy or microfilm checks, drafts, or money orders, *both* sides of the checks *must* be reproduced unless the reverse sides are blank.

Detailed information concerning Public Law 91-508 can be obtained by requesting from the United States Department of the Treasury a publication prepared by the Office of the General Counsel of the Treasury entitled, "Currency and Foreign Transactions Reporting Act – Statute, Regulations and Forms." Requests should be addressed to the Deputy Assistant Secretary (Enforcement) the Department of the Treasury, Washington, D.C. 20220.

12

Illustrative Cases Employing Source and Application of Funds Schedules

To Corroborate Kickback Case
(Tempera Case)

On March 5, 1982, a trial jury in Suffolk County, New York (Smithtown) returned a guilty verdict on multiple counts of perjury against Mr. Lou V. Tempera, former county Commissioner of Labor. The perjury indictment was returned in 1981 following the defendant's denials before a grand jury that he had received kickbacks from the recipients of Federal Comprehensive Employment Training Act (CETA) grants that he had approved.

The prosecutors were James J. O'Rourke (now in private practice), who was at that time Chief of the Special Investigation Unit in the office of then District Attorney Patrick Henry (presently a Judge in the New York Supreme Court) and Mark Cohen (presently a Chief Assistant District Attorney). They recognized the difficulties inherent in convincing a jury "beyond a reasonable doubt" that a public official (with no prior criminal record) received kickbacks in currency when the primary evidence of said kickbacks consisted of the uncorroborated testimony of the individuals who made the kickbacks.

The difficulties were further compounded by the fact that the payors of the kickbacks had been charged with related criminal offenses.

Detectives Stephen Enoch and Steven Drielak, employed by the Suffolk County District Attorney's office and under the guidance of the prosecutors, had gathered considerable information concerning the defendant's expenditures over a period of several years, the same years that the defendant was allegedly "on the take."

As a result, the prosecutors decided to introduce into evidence an array of documents concerning the defendant's expenditures. The purpose of offering the evidence was to show that the defendant was spending more money each year than he had available from known sources, thereby creating an inference that he must necessarily have had funds available from unknown sources. All this evidence was summarized through Nossen's expert testimony.

The prosecutor was then able to offer to the jury *corroboration* of the direct evidence of payments of kickbacks to the defendant, thereby enhancing the credibility of the witnesses who paid them. Following the guilty verdict, several jurors remarked to the press that the "expenditures" evidence was a significant factor during their deliberations.

This was the first time that the IRS "net worth" and/or "source and application of funds" technique, stripped of its tax complexities, was utilized as corroborative evidence in the trial of a non-tax financial crime.

This success in the Tempera trial has resulted in the widespread use of similar techniques by criminal investigators and prosecutors determined to "follow the money trail." Similar cases are described in subsequent sections of this chapter.

The following schedule is similar to the schedule introduced into evidence in the Tempera trial. Additional facts of the case are covered in the newspaper articles which follow and in an article from *The Notre Dame Law Review,* Volume 58, No. 5, June, 1983, which is included as Appendix A.

TEMPERA CASE
SOURCE AND APPLICATION OF FUNDS
1977-1980

	1977	1978	1979	1980	TOTAL
SOURCES OF FUNDS:					
Suffolk County Salary	29,789.47	28,550.13	29,973.47	32,407.55	
New York State Salary	1,486.43	1,347.93	712.42	1,502.82	
Municipal Bond Interest	12,072.12	15,610.00	19,997.50	26,335.00	
Savings Account Interest	1,170.92	686.75	728.42	843.93	
Proceeds of Mortg.-Blue Bell Lane	29,588.16				
Business Income	5,054.08	14,800.00	14,800.00	14,800.00	
Rental Income	2,400.00	4,800.00	4,800.00	4,800.00	
Proceeds of Insurance Claim			1,850.00		
TOTAL SOURCES OF FUNDS	81,561.18	65,794.81	72,861.81	80,689.30	300,907.10
EXPENDITURES:					
Increase in Bank Account Balances:					
European American Bank	461.14	(235.42)	(20,174.05)	19,692.00	
SC F.S.& L. #10-10-119304-2	13,512.99	171.13	(593.34)	(12,879.30)	
SC F.S.& L. #10-10-119302-6	1,092.25	223.65	493.35	(2,330.83)	
Purchase of Municipal Bonds	80,655.53	42,136.66	80,210.94	81,377.91	
Matured Bond	(25,000.00)				
Purchase of 34-Blue Bell Lane	36,392.28				
Improvements to 34-Blue Bell Lane	5,000.00	2,800.00			
Purchase of 2 Grand Prix Automobiles	9,576.50				
Investment in IRA's:					
Acct # 785-65848		75.00		1,925.00	
Acct # 785-65849		75.00		400.00	
Purch of Cert. of Deposit #897-00209				3,000.00	
Increase in Mortgage Escrow Acct. Bal	477.88	(1,967.81)	195.33	1,920.34	
Purch of Babylon Cemetery Ass'n Plot		500.00			
Paymts on Mort 121 Village Line (prin	809.59	723.64	832.08	878.99	
Real Est Taxes & Mortgage Int Paymts	3,492.84	5,727.75	3,937.12	2,020.18	
Income Taxes Paid (In Excess of W/H)	952.20	6,809.27	744.58	2,325.28	
Insurance Premiums	1,012.00	900.00	1,208.00	1,427.00	
Utilities	2,773.59	3,122.52	4,522.74	2,704.50	
Furniture	883.75	1,107.01	5,097.15		
Expenses Related to Rental Property	5,273.00	6,276.00			
Christmas Club				115.00	
Increase in Bank Account Balances:					
Bank of Babylon-Checking	410.29	(373.37)	(6.24)	37.79	
Bank of Babylon-Savings	3,417.91	(3,287.14)	6.65	6.99	
Mortgage Payments-34 Blue Bell Lane		4,812.00	5,120.66	5,122.21	
Living Expenses	0.00	0.00	0.00	0.00	
TOTAL EXPENDITURES	141,193.74	69,595.89	81,594.97	107,743.06	400,127.66
EXPENDITURES IN EXCESS OF	(59,632.56)	(3,801.08)	(8,733.16)	(27,053.76)	(99,220.56)
KNOWN SOURCES OF FUNDS					

Tactic Used In Tempera Case Studied

By John McDonald

Smithtown—The conviction of former Suffolk Labor Commissioner Lou V. Tempera is drawing the attention of prosecutors from around the state because it is the first political-corruption case in 50 years in which the prosecutor used a "net worth case" tactic in state court.

Tempera was convicted on Friday of five counts of perjury. Jurors have said that the net worth case tactic was one of the deciding factors during their five days of deliberations. In presenting the net worth case, a prosecution witness testified that Tempera spent $99,000 more than he legally earned from 1977 through 1980. The figure was later revised down to $33,000.

Gregory Carlock, coordinator of the Economic Crime Council, an arm of the New York State District Attorneys Association, said the council is planning a seminar on the tactic for next month for prosecutors from around the state. The two Suffolk prosecutors who worked on the Tempera case, James J. O'Rourke, chief of the special investigations unit and Mark Cohen, the unit's deputy chief will be the main speakers at the seminar.

"This tactic can be used in a variety of cases including bribery, larceny, drugs and tax evasion," Carlock said, "as long as the receipt of money is an issue in the trial." He said that O'Rourke and Cohen were being asked to the seminar because, "We want to take advantage of their expertise. We'll be asking them about the practical application of the tactic."

In an interview yesterday, O'Rourke and Cohen said that the difficulty in presenting the net worth case was in gathering information on Tempera's income and expenditures. It involved "thousands" of hours of investigation and included collecting both Tempera's income records and his bills from a wide range of sources including his home-heating-oil supplier, furniture dealers and automobile dealers and all of his bank records.

When using the tactic in the future, O'Rourke said that he hopes to have the defendant's federal tax returns. In the Tempera case the federal returns were first given to the prosecution during the trial. The federal returns contributed heavily to the prosecution having to revise its $99,000 estimate down to $33,000. Federal returns, O'Rourke said, can be obtained if accountants prepare them. In addition, the Tempera case led to more financial records becoming available to prosecutors. The Appellate Division of State Supreme Court ruled that financial disclosure statements filed by high ranking Suffolk officials with county's Board of Public Disclosure can be subpoenaed by a grand jury.

The use of the net worth case tactic, "will be one of the biggest issues of our appeal," said Tempera's lawyer Stephen Scaring. "I believe it [the verdict] can be reversed on that issue alone." He said the evidence used in the net worth case confused the jury, which disregarded both estimates and came up with its own estimate, that Tempera spent $70,000 more than his legal income, Scaring said a juror told him. Another juror who discussed the case with Newsday, confirmed that.

Finance Expert Details Tempera Spending

By John McDonald

Hauppauge—Suffolk Labor Commissioner Lou V. Tempera spent $99,220 more than he earned from 1977 through 1980, according to testimony by a private expert in investigating economic crime.

The testimony in State Supreme Court was part of the prosecution's attempt to prove that Tempera committed perjury when he denied to a county grand jury that he had accepted more than $100,000 in payoffs in connection with the awarding of manpower training contracts.

Richard Nossen of Midlothiar, Va., a retired assistant director of the Internal Revenue Service criminal investigation division, said he based the estimate on his study of the 462 exhibits that have gone into evidence.

Earlier, a second hearing was held on the health of Tempera's wife, Dorothy. On Wednesday, Acting State Supreme Court Justice Harry Seidell had excused her from having to testify, citing health reasons. She was to have been in court yesterday while Seidell considered whether to have her questioned in his chambers, but she did not appear. Her physician, Richard Sweeney, testified that her condition, a combination of a rare blood disease and stress, had worsened and that he had ordered her to stay in bed.

Assistant District Attorney James J. O'Rourke withdrew his demand to question her after the defense provided a list of her bank accounts and disclosed that her total salary from

1972 to 1980 was $6,000. Seidell ruled that several other questions O'Rourke had wanted answered were improper because they appeared to violate the Temperas' right to marital privacy.

O'Rourke is using a "net worth" tactic, attempting to show that Tempera spent more than he legally earned, to support allegations that Tempera received payoffs.

Defense attorney Steven Scaring repeatedly objected as O'Rourke questioned Nossen, claiming that O'Rourke has not shown the court Tempera's assets prior to the four-year period being examined, a possible explanation for his source of extra money. Seidell permitted Nossen's testimony, but prohibited O'Rourke from using a 3-by-5-foot chart, mounted on wood, as a guide for the jury to follow the testimony.

Nossen outlined Tempera's expenses, including his utility bills; automobile, furniture and municipal-bond purchases; taxes, and insurance costs. Tempera's sources of income included his net county salary, his salary as a consultant to the State Legislature, interest on his municipal bonds and savings, and income from his private consulting firm and from a house he rents out.

The estimate of Tempera's finances did not include any expenses for food, clothing or household expenses. Nossen said that over the four-year period, Tempera's net income totaled $300,907 and his expenses totaled $400,127. Scaring is to cross-examine Nossen today.

○ *To Corroborate Embezzlement Charges* ○
(King Case)

One of the many advantages of the use of expenditures evidence as a corroborative technique is that the amount of money involved can, in many cases, be a relatively nominal amount. An example is the King case in DeKalb County, Atlanta, Georgia, which went to trial in 1990. Jimmy King, an administrative assistant to the DeKalb County Superior Court, was in charge of coin-operated copying machines in the County Clerk's office during 1987 and 1988.

A routine audit disclosed that more than $125,000 appeared to be missing from the copy machine revenue over a period of several years which included the years when King had control. The County District Attorney, Bob Wilson, did not allege that King was responsible for the entire theft but did charge that some of the money was taken by King.

While there was considerable direct evidence available to the prosecutor to warrant King's indictment, Wilson felt that it would be advantageous if he could present at trial corroborative evidence that King had spent more money during the years in question than he had available from known sources.

Based on evidence gathered during the course of the investigation by Wilson's staff, Nossen and one of his associates, Joe Pagani (a former Internal Revenue Service colleague), testified. Their testimony established that King had less than $282.00 per month available in 1987 and less than $232.00 per month available in 1988 from known sources to pay for food, clothing, auto expenses, entertainment, medical expenses, and other day-to-day living expenses for himself and his elderly father. This evidence created a reasonable inference that he must necessarily have had an "unknown" source of income. The obvious conclusion was that the unknown source of income was from the skim from the coin-operated copying machines.

While King's total expenditures were nominal, it is interesting to note that neither Nossen's nor Pagani's computations were challenged by defense counsel. *There was no cross examination.*

The following Source and Application of Funds Schedule is similar to one of the schedules utilized by Nossen and Pagani during the trial. News clippings related to this case follow.

JAMES D. KING, JR.
SOURCE AND APPLICATION OF FUNDS
1987-1988

	1987		1988	
SOURCES OF FUNDS:				
W-2 Gross Income		26,649.04		28,909.79
Less:				
Federal Withholding	4,949.60		5,480.07	
State Withholding	1,370.47		1,514.55	
Social Security	1,905.41		2,171.12	
County Pension	666.11		722.56	
Loan Payments	1,269.00		1,222.00	
Health Insurance	281.46		344.52	
Accidental Death			7.88	
Life Insurance	55.42	(10,497.47)	56.29	(11,518.99)
Net Income		16,151.57		17,390.80
Add:				
Fed.& St.Inc.Tax Refunds		759.64		1,109.07
Proceeds from Cr Un Loan		2,000.00		
TOTAL SOURCES OF FUNDS		18,911.21		18,499.87
EXPENDITURES:				
Checking Acct Withdrawals	21,957.31		18,342.82	
Rent: 1/2 yr pd with cash	2,860.00		2,940.00	
Power: 1/2 yr pd with cash	24.91		94.56	
Phone: 1/2 yr pd with cash	143.70			
Cable: 1/2 yr pd with cash	154.25		107.75	
Auto down paym.in cash	2,000.00		1,000.00	
Increase in sav.acct bal.			3,750.00	
Inc in checking acct bal.	401.74		102.62	
TOTAL EXPENDITURES		27,541.91		26,337.75
EXPENDITURES IN EXCESS OF KNOWN SOURCES OF FUNDS		(8,630.70)		(7,837.88)

*Note: Expenditures do not include food, gasoline, entertainment,
or a variety of other miscellaneous expenses.

★★★ WED., JULY 4, 1990   The Atlanta Inn

DeKalb employee found guilty of theft

Case concerns coin-operated copy machines

By Anne Cowles
Staff writer

An administrative assistant to DeKalb County's Superior Court clerk was found guilty Tuesday of stealing money from coin-operated copy machines while he was in charge of their operation in 1987 and 1988.

Jimmy King, 40, could face a maximum 15 years in prison. Sentencing is tentatively scheduled for July 30 before DeKalb Superior Court Judge Carol W. Hunstein.

The investigation into theft of copy machine proceeds is not con te and could lead to crin....al charges against other individuals, said DeKalb District Attorney Bob Wilson.

"There is no question [that] over $125,000 is missing from the copy machines from 1981 to 1988," Mr. Wilson said. "In convicting Jimmy King, we never contended he stole it all, and in fact, we know he did not."

No dollar amount was alleged in the indictment against King, but at least $50,000 of the $125,000 was stolen from the copy machine proceeds when King was directly in charge of them in 1987 and 1988.

King's attorney, Douglas Peters, said his client plans to appeal the verdict, which a jury of seven women and five men

John Spink/Staff

Jimmy King (left) examines a ledger shown to him by DeKalb District Attorney Bob Wilson.

reached after 3 ½ hours of deliberation.

In closing arguments, Mr. Peters blamed DeKalb Superior Court Clerk Whitfield C. Smith for creating the impression among his employees that the copy machine proceeds were "his money" when it actually should be turned over to the county each month.

"Whit Smith is not only the elected public official [in that office], he is Jimmy's boss," Mr. Peters said. "He is an attorney and a member of the Bar.

Everyone considered this [copy machine proceeds] the clerk's money. ... They were told to hide that money when the auditors came in."

But Mr. Wilson told the jury, "Whit Smith is not on trial today. ... Whit Smith has his problems and you've heard just some of them in this courtroom."

Mr. Smith, criticized by a grand jury in November 1988 for keeping a secret cash account with copy machine proceeds, has since repaid the county $17,500.

Theft suspect newly affluent, DA tells jury

Ex-court aide on trial in DeKalb

By Donna Williams Lewis
Staff writer

An administrative assistant to DeKalb's Superior Court clerk found "a new prosperity" after being put in charge of copy machines, a prosecutor told a jury Thursday in the aide's trial on charges of stealing copy machine proceeds.

"Suddenly, he seemed to have more available cash than he used to have," DeKalb District Attorney Robert E. Wilson said of Jimmy King. "He finds a new prosperity."

Mr. King, 40, was fired after being indicted in February on charges of stealing money from the coin-operated copy machines in the court clerk's office over a four-year period.

No dollar amount has been cited, but Mr. Wilson has said that about $100,000 is missing from copy machine proceeds from 1981 through 1988 — including roughly $50,000 when Mr. King was directly in charge of the machines in 1987 and 1988.

The prosecution does not contend that Mr. King stole all of the money, "but we will show you that he stole some," Mr. Wilson told the jury during opening arguments.

Mr. King's lifestyle changed only because he met his wife, who "is a little more sophisticated" than Mr. King, said his attorney, Douglas N. Peters. Mr. King was only following the orders of his boss, Superior Court Clerk Whitfield Smith, in dealing with the copy machines, Mr. Peters told the jury.

Employees, including Mr. Smith, cashed checks and bought soft drinks with copy machine proceeds from time to time, he said.

"This thieving that's been described to you started in 1981, not in 1985 when Mr. King took

Jimmy King
Fired DeKalb court aide listens to testimony Thursday.

over [the machines]," Mr. Peters said. "At least when Mr. King took over, he said, 'Let's at least take it off the counter. Let's at least put it in the drawer.' "

The investigation began after Mr. King gave a photocopy of a document referred to as "the red ledger book" to his friend, Lee Stanley, Mr. Smith's longtime political opponent, who informed the district attorney's office, Mr. Wilson said.

Mr. Stanley "held out some hope of reward for Mr. King," Mr. Wilson said, such as making him a No. 2 person in the office if Mr. Stanley was elected.

Mr. Smith, criticized by a grand jury in November 1988 for keeping a secret cash account with copy machine proceeds, has since repaid the county $17,500.

To Justify Civil Forfeiture Action
(Sparano Case)

Richard Sparano pleaded guilty to conspiracy to manufacture and distribute cocaine and methamphetamine, racketeering, and income tax evasion. He received a substantial prison sentence.

Sparano and the prosecutor were unable to reach an agreement, however, regarding the extent to which his assets, presumably acquired with the proceeds from his illegal activities, should be forfeited. The civil forfeiture matters were ultimately tried by a jury.

The jury ordered all assets forfeited to the government. The jury's decision was appealed on several grounds. However, the primary issue was whether Sparano's accumulation of cash and substantial ownership of real estate were directly or indirectly derived from his admitted illegal drug activities.

Anthony Higham and Raina Siskin, investigators with the Narcotics Task Force of the New Jersey Attorney General's office, prepared a Source and Application of Funds analysis on Sparano for the years 1982 through 1987. The schedule was admitted into evidence during the course of Higham's testimony. The analysis disclosed that Sparano's expenditures were substantially in excess of his legitimate sources of funds.

The Appellate Division of the New Jersey Superior Court affirmed the jury verdict, based in large part on the investigators' Source and Application of Funds computation. In its ruling the Court stated that "there need not be a 'direct' connection between racketeering profits and the acquired property sought to be forfeited, so long as the state proves that the property was acquired by funds equivalent to the fruits of the criminal activity."

The Court also stated that "the state endeavored to prove that the defendant's expenditures during the period covered by the indictment far exceeded his known legitimate sources of income, while the defendant contended that he and his wife, Donna, had generated considerable (although not necessarily reported) cash income from legitimate business ventures. Suffice it to say that there was more than sufficient evidence presented at the eight-day trial to permit the finding that defendant's income far exceeded his earnings from legitimate sources."

A copy of the summary schedule similar to the one prepared by the investigators is shown below. News clipping are also reproduced.

```
SUMMARY OF SOURCE AND APPLICATION OF FUNDS
RICHARD AND DONNA SPARANO
1982-1987
```

YEAR	SOURCE OF FUNDS	APPLICATION OF FUNDS	YEARLY FUNDS AVAILABLE	CUMMULATIVE FUNDS AVAIL.
1982	21,050.00	40,242.71	(19,192.71)	(19,192.71)
1983	18,041.00	10,799.25	7,241.75	(11,950.96)
1984	55,265.84	44,560.12	10,705.72	(1,245.24)
1985	75,375.34	109,664.13	(34,288.79)	(35,534.03)
1986	122,978.85	218,628.57	(95,649.72)	(131,183.75)
1987	294,839.00	517,161.72	(222,322.72)	(353,506.47)
TOTAL	587,550.03	941,056.50	(353,506.47)	

THE STAR-LEDGER, Tuesday, July 9, 1991

State can confiscate ill-gotten gains without direct tie to criminal activity
Racketeer rebuffed on appeal of loss of his home and condo

By TOM HESTER

The state can confiscate a racketeer's property even though it was not directly purchased with money obtained through criminal activity, a state appeals court held yesterday in a precedent-setting ruling.

The decision by the three-judge panel clears the way for the Attorney General's Office to auction the single-family house and condominium owned by a Hamilton man who pleaded guilty to operating a drug ring in Mercer County between 1982 and 1985. In addition, the state can claim $298,000 in cash confiscated from him.

The ruling is the result of an unsuccessful appeal brought by the drug dealer, Richard Sparano, 35, who is serving four to 11 years in prison for pleading guilty to manufacturing and distributing drugs, racketeering and tax evasion.

The plea bargain also required Sparano to testify against his brother, Dennis, 45, of Hamilton. The elder Sparano also pleaded guilty and was sentenced to eight to 16 years for his role in the drug ring. He had to forfeit $100,000 in property to the state.

Richard Sparano turned to the appeals court when a Superior Court jury in Trenton found that the houses and money were obtained "directly or indirectly as a result of his admitted violation of the New Jersey racketeering law."

Sparano appealed that his Kristin Way home, a condominium he owns at Grandville Arms on Silver Court and the cash were purchased or obtained through his legitimate businesses, a video game arcade in Hamilton and a liquor store in Trenton.

The home is valued at $225,000 to $250,000, according to Deputy Attorney General Jay H. Hindman, who prosecuted the case, and the condo is worth $100,000.

An opinion written by Judge Edwin H. Stern and supported by Judges Richard S. Cohen and Virginia Long supported the jury's decision.

"We hold," Stern stated, "that there need not be a 'direct' connection between racketeering profits and the acquired property sought to be forfeited, so long as the state proves that the property was acquired by funds equivalent to the fruits of the criminal activity."

"This is the first published opinion in New Jersey dealing with racketeering forfeiture provisions under the racketeering statute," said Hindman. "There is a dearth of New Jersey law regarding racketeering forfeiture."

Sparano's attorney, Mark W. Catanzaro of Mt. Holly, was not immediately available for comment. The unanimous ruling means the state Supreme Court does not have to review the decision.

Sparano contended Superior Court Judge David J. Schroth improperly instructed the jury. Schroth told the jurors that when a person uses illegal money for living expenses, it can be considered an asset, even if it was bought with money that could be traced to legitimate sources. The theory is that without the illegal income, the person would not have been able to preserve his other legitimate resources to purchase the property.

Stern, Cohen and Long concluded Schroth acted properly.

Reviewing the trial, the judges noted Dennis Sparano testified the video arcade and liquor store were unsuccessful and that his brother "lived good," "wanted for nothing" and lived off "the drug business."

The judges also noted Anthony Higham, an investigator and accountant for the state Narcotics Task Force, concluded that Richard Sparano had spent $353,000 in excess of his known income.

"The primary issue in the trial was whether defendant's interest in the $298,000 cash and the real properties were directly or indirectly derived from his admitted illegal drug business," Stern stated. "The state endeavored to prove that defendant's expenditures during the period covered by the indictment far exceeded his known legitimate sources of income, while defendant contended that he and his wife, Donna, had generated considerable (although not necessarily reported) cash income from legitimate business ventures.

"Suffice it to say," Stern added, "that there was more than sufficient evidence presented at the eight-day trial to permit the finding that defendant's income far exceeded his earnings from legitimate sources."

The Trentonian   Friday, February 14, 1992

Drug lord OKs deal he fought to overturn

■ Dennis Sparano pleaded guilty a 2nd time.

By TONY WILSON
The Trentonian

Dennis Sparano is a drug kingpin who apparently can't decide whether he's guilty or innocent.

In 1989, Sparano pleaded guilty to cocaine, racketeering and tax evasion charges. He was sentenced to 16 years behind bars.

But two years later, Sparano changed his mind. He said he wasn't guilty and really didn't understand the terms of the plea bargain.

The case worked its way through the appellate courts, where a judge decided that agreement could be overturned.

The trial was supposed to start yesterday.

But once again, Sparano pleaded guilty to the charges and agreed to a plea bargain with state prosecutors — the same deal he earlier rejected.

Under the agreement, the 46-year-old Sparano must serve at least eight years of a 16-year prison sentence.

He must also forfeit more than $1 million in cash and real estate holdings that were derived largely through his racketeering.

In turn, the state will set up a $110,000 trust fund — from the forfeiture money — for Sparano's two children, a boy now 19, and a 16-year-old girl. The trust fund was also part of the 1989 plea agreement.

Had Sparano gone to trial and been convicted, he could have been sentenced to a life behind bars. Under the life term, he would have had to serve at least 25 years before being eligible for parole.

Prosecutors say Sparano was the brains behind a multi-million dollar racketeering conspiracy that sold large amounts of cocaine and manufactured and distributed methamphetamine, or speed, in central New Jersey.

> Under the agreement, Sparano must serve at least eight years in prison.

Sparano first pleaded guilty after his brother and co-defendant, Richard Sparano, admitted his own guilt and implicated his sibling and two others.

Jay Hindman, assistant state attorney general, said the new plea agreement was reached with Sparano and the defendant's attorney, John Furlong, on Wednesday

Jury selection was set to begin yesterday.

Hindman said the trust for Sparano's children will be funded in part from $600,000 in proceeds from the sale of Sparano's Bon Vivant business complex on Route 130 in Washington Township.

That complex was acquired largely with racketeering money.

When asked why drug-tainted money should be used to set up a trust fund for Sparano's children, Hindman replied:

"Assuming it was right then (in the 1989 agreement), why wouldn't it be right now?"

Superior Court Judge David J. Schroth described the agreement as "generous to Mr. Sparano."

Sparano is scheduled to be sentenced on March 6. Until then, he will remain free on $300,000 bail.

To Justify Civil Seizure Action
(Wilson Case)

The subject in this case is described by the FBI Agent in an affidavit in support of a seizure warrant issued by the U.S. District Court, Northern District of California, as a "participant in a cocaine distribution conspiracy." Seizure action has been successfully undertaken against the subject's residence as a result of alleged violations of Title 21, U.S. Code, Section 881.

The first section of FBI agent Stephen Dybsky's affidavit contains the usual factual material, i.e., the identification and background of the agent, the alleged illegal drug activities of the alleged violator, and information obtained from informants. The concluding section of the affidavit is entitled: "Source and Application of Funds and Financial Analysis." It contains the following:

1. The use of a Source and Application of Funds schedule for a three-year period. The schedule is attached to the seizure warrant as an exhibit;

2. The identification of Nossen, who prepared the schedule, and his qualifications; and

3. A summary of Nossen's conclusions establishing the extent to which the subject's expenditures exceeded his known sources of income for each of the three years in question.

Once again, expenditures evidence presented in the form of a Source and Application of Funds computation has been used to corroborate evidence of an alleged illegal activity. The property, allegedly acquired by its owner with funds obtained from illegal activities, has been forfeited to the United States government. The full text of the seizure warrant affidavit follows as well as news clippings related to this case. The source and application of funds schedule is attached to the seizure warrant.

WILLIAM T. McGIVERN, JR.
United States Attorney

LIZABETH A. McKIBBEN
Assistant United States Attorney
Northern District of California
450 Golden Gate Avenue
Box 36132
San Francisco, California   94102
Telephone: (415) 556-0750

3-91 0136

JSB

Attorneys for Plaintiff

UNITED STATES DISTRICT COURT

NORTHERN DISTRICT OF CALIFORNIA

UNITED STATES OF AMERICA,)	
)	
Plaintiff,)	
)	No.
v.)	
)	
5645 Bacon Road)	
Oakland, California)	**A F F I D A V I T**
County of Alameda)	
)	
Defendant.)	

I, Stephen R. Dybsky, being duly sworn states as
follows: I am employed as a Special Agent of the Federal Bureau
of Investigation (FBI) and have been so employed for over twenty
years. From March of 1982 until April, 1989 I was assigned to
the San Francisco Organized Crime Enforcement Task Force
(OCDETF) working with various local and federal agencies and the
United States Attorneys Office in the investigation of large
scale narcotics trafficking organizations. As part of this
experience, I participated in the management of investigations
of large scale bay area cocaine distribution networks including
the Julio Zavala/Alavajo Carvajal-Minota organization, and most

UNITED STATES DISTRICT COURT

NORTHERN DISTRICT OF CALIFORNIA

UNITED STATES OF AMERICA	)	NO. CR-3-91 0136
Plaintiff,	)	<u>SEIZURE WARRANT</u>
v.	)	
5645 BACON ROAD	)	
OAKLAND, CALIFORNIA,	)	
Defendant.	)	

TO ANY SPECIAL AGENT OF THE FEDERAL BUREAU OF INVESTIGATION OR OTHER FEDERAL OFFICER:

Affidavit having been made before me by Stephen Dybsky, Special Agent, Federal Bureau of Investigation, that he has reason to believe that the above-described Real Property was used in violation of Title 21, United States Code, Section 881, and that said Real Property is located in the Northern District of California, and that the Court being satisfied that there are sufficient facts and circumstances establishing probable cause to believe that the above-described Real Property was used in violation of Title 21, United States Code, Section 881, and that grounds for the issuance of the Seizure Warrant exists as stated in the supporting affidavit, therefore, pursuant to Title 21, United States Code, Section 881.

YOU ARE HEREBY COMMANDED to seize within a period of ten (10) days, the above described property, serving this warrant and seizing said property in the daytime (6:00 a.m. to 10:00 p.m.), recently the Rudolph Henderson/Alvaro Becerra organization. Both of these investigations included lengthy Title III wire taps, and of the execution of numerous search warrants. The two investigations resulted in the arrest and conviction of over fifty defendants, and the seizure of several million dollars in assets.

Since April of 1989 your affiant has been responsible for the supervision and management of the FBI's Forfeiture Asset Seizure Team (FAST) of the San Francisco Division. During this period of time, i.e. April of 1989 to the present, the San Francisco Forfeiture Asset Seizure Team has been responsible for the processing of paperwork for approximately $20 million of targeted assets.

The information contained in this affidavit is based upon my participation in the Stephen Wilson investigation, my discussion with other FBI and Internal Revenue Service Agents participating in the investigation, interviews I have conducted, and upon my review of reports, wire tap transcripts, surveillance logs, financial records, and other records prepared or obtained as a result of the Wilson investigation. I incorporate in full herein by reference and make available to the court for its review the Title III affidavits of Special Agent Robert Moore and Special Agent Carl Podsiadly (Exhibits A and B); the Master Affidavit for search warrants of Special Agent Robert Moore (Exhibit C), and the results of the "Source and Application of Funds" analysis of retired Internal Revenue Service Agent Richard A. Nossen (Exhibit D).

The following affidavit is being submitted in support of a seizure warrant for real property known as 5645 Bacon Road, Oakland, California, and is subject to seizure pursuant to Title 21, United States Code, Sections 881 (a)(6) and (7).

In early 1986 Stephen Wilson was negotiating for the purchase of the defendant property through an estate representative. In the course of negotiations Stephen Wilson made a $15,000.00 "earnest money" deposit, which he subsequently increased to $40,000.00. On March 18, 1986 Stephen Wilson informed the estate representative that the purchase of the defendant property was to be made by his designated nominee. At this time Stephen Wilson named his nominee to be George Smith and Smith's wife, Darlene. At this time George Smith made a down payment of $276,455.32, which was put towards the purchase price of $705,000.00, less credits due to buyer. The closing papers reflected the fact that Stephen Wilson's $40,000.00 was assigned to George Smith to be added to Smith's down payment for the property. Subsequent to the sale Stephen Wilson's name was not reflected on the title for the property, only George Smith and his wife. Approximately nine months later in December, 1986, Stephen Wilson purchased 5645 Bacon Road, Oakland, California from George Smith for approximately $416,000.00. Wilson's down payment for this December 1986 transaction was $66,120.00. As of December 16, 1986 Stephen Wilson, an unmarried man was the owner of record for the defendant property. During the nine month interim period between the two aforementioned transactions, Stephen Wilson spent several thousand dollars on renovation and upgrading of the defendant property.

On March 19, 1987 an "effect of deed" was recorded that changed the title of the defendant property from Stephen Wilson to Trousdale Investments. Investigation has determined that Trousdale Investment is a business name used by Stephen Wilson.

The following is a legal description of the defendant property, located at 5645 Bacon Road, obtained from the Office of County Clerk, County of Alameda, California:

Parcel One:

Portion of the land shown on "Record of Survey Portion of American Trust Company Property, Oakland, Alameda County, California", filed April 13, 1951 in Licensed Survey Book 3, Page 14, Alameda County Records, described as follows: Beginning at a point on the center line of Bacon Road, distant thereon 335.181 feet southwesterly from the southwestern line of Skyline Boulevard, as the said road and boulevard are shown on said "Record of Survey", from said point of beginning the center of a curve, with a radius of 240 feet, forming a portion of said center line of Bacon Road, South 49° 13' 44" east distant 240 feet; thence from said point of beginning southwesterly along the arc of said mentioned curve to the left, a distance of 24.17 feet to a point from which the center of a compound curve with a radius of 100 feet, bears south 55° east; thence southwesterly along the arc of said last mentioned curve to the left, a distance of 15.83 feet to a point from which the center of said last mentioned curve bears south 64° 04' 09" east; thence leaving said center line of Bacon Road North 75° west 238 feet; thence north 64° 17' 33" west 421.42 feet; thence north 39° 13' 22" east 70 feet thence north 53° 09' 09" east, 183.32 feet to a point on the northeastern boundary line of said tract of land; thence running along said northeastern boundary line, south 45° 07' 52" east, 451.385 feet and south 64° 43' 24" east, 134.44 feet to the point of beginning. To be known and designated as Homesite No. 111.

<u>Parcel Two:</u>

An easement for road, sewer and public utility purposes, appurtenant to and for the benefit of Parcel One above described over and along all that portion of Bacon Road, as shown on said "Record of Survey", mentioned in Parcel One above, lying without Parcel One above described and over all other roads as shown on said record of survey, and on "Record of Survey", portion of the American Trust Company Property, Oakland, Alameda County, California, filed July 19, 1947, in licensed survey book, pages 37, 38, 39, and 40, Alameda County Records; and also an easement for road, sewer and public purposes appurtenant to and for the benefit of Parcel One above described over and along any other roads in lands embraced in any further and future tract of tracts contiguous to the land described in said record of survey hereinabove referred to, or to tracts contiguous to such further tracts, provided such land embraced in such further tract or tracts, tracts are now owned by American Trust Company and from a part of that portion of the parcel of land firstly described in the deed by Syndicate Merriwood Co., Ltd., to American Trust Company, dated August 22, 1946, recorded August 30, 1946, Book 4934, Page 304, Series No. TT/077284, Alameda County Records, that lies easterly of the general western line of the land shown on said records of survey.

HISTORY OF CRIMINAL INVESTIGATION

RE STEPHEN WILSON and DENISE SMITH

Attached Exhibits A (Title III affidavit of SA Robert Moore), B (Title III affidavit of SA Carl Podsiadly), and C (Master Affidavit for Search Warrants of SA Robert Moore) incorporated herein by reference describe the activities of Guillermo Diaz, Janet C. Lossa, Joe DePalm, Stephen Wilson, Denise Smith, Harold Londono, Jan Hightower and others, and detail the probable cause as to their participation in a conspiracy to distribute cocaine. The investigation of this cocaine distribution conspiracy began in early 1987 and has continued to the present. During the course of this investigation in December, 1988 several subjects were arrested including Guillermo Diaz, Janet Lossa, Joe DePalm, and Harold Londono. Subsequent to their arrest Diaz, Lossa, DePalm and Londono pled guilty and were sentenced. Guillermo Diaz pled guilty to one count of Title 21, U.S.C., Section 846, Distribution of Cocaine and was sentenced to 121 months imprisonment and to a three year term of supervised release. Janet Lossa pled guilty to one count of Title 21, U.S.C., Section 946, Distribution of Cocaine and was sentenced to 97 months imprisonment and to a three year term of supervised

release. Joseph DePalm pled guilty to one count of Title 21, U.S.C., Section 846, Distribution of Cocaine and sentenced to 97 months imprisonment and to a three year term of supervised release. Harold Londono pled guilty to one count of Title 21, U.S.C., Section 846, Distribution of Cocaine and sentenced to 63 **months imprisonment and to a three year term of supervised release.**

During the course of the investigation it was determined that Guillermo Diaz and Janet Lossa were two principals in a cocaine distribution conspiracy. Through physical surveillance and electronic surveillance, i.e. telephone intercepts, it was determined that Steve Wilson was a **participant in the cocaine distribution conspiracy. The first indication that the investigating agents had that Wilson was involved in the conspiracy occurred on May 13, 1988 when Wilson telephonically contacted Diaz and said he wanted to talk to Diaz.** Arrangements were made for Diaz to meet Wilson at Wilson's residence located at 650 Trestle Glen, Oakland, California. At approximately 3:20 p.m. later that day Diaz was observed by FBI surveillance agents arriving at and entering the residence of Wilson located at 650 Trestle Glen, Oakland, California. Between May 13, 1988 and June 8, 1988 numerous contacts occurred between Wilson and Diaz through the use of pagers, Diaz's car telephone and Diaz's home telephone (see pages 26-28 of Exhibit C).

On July 20, 1988 Guillermo Diaz, Janet Lossa, and Stephen Wilson were observed by FBI surveillance agents meeting at Vanessi's Restaurant located at 1177 California Street, San Francisco, California.

On August 4, 1988 Guillermo Diaz called his wife, Kathleen Richmond at their residence and during the course of the conversation Richmond asked Diaz if he was seeing Steve Wilson, to which Diaz replied he did not want to rush him, and that he would call Steve Wilson later. (see Exhibit C page 42)

On August 10, 1988 Diaz contacted Janet Lossa and during their conversation Diaz told Lossa that Stevie Wilson did not want to do anything right now because the price was not right. (see Exhibit C page 42).

On August 13, 1988 Diaz called Janet Lossa and during their discussion Lossa asked Diaz to contact Stevie Wilson, and for Diaz to determine what "number" is unworkable for Steve. Diaz told Lossa he would contact Stevie the following Monday and he would meet with Lossa on Monday (see Exhibit C page 43).

Beginning on September 8, 1988 and continuing through September 13, 1988 numerous contacts were made between Steve Wilson and Guillermo Diaz, and between Diaz and Janet Lossa (see Exhibit C page 47-51).

Your affiant believes that the conversations summarized in the aforementioned referenced pages in Exhibit C involve an effort on the part of Steve Wilson to negotiate a cocaine transaction with Janet Lossa through Guillermo Diaz, Lossa's source for the cocaine being unidentified individuals in southern California.

In October, 1988 Title III telephone intercepts

reflect a continuation of the effort on the part of Diaz and Lossa to negotiate a cocaine transaction which at least a portion of which included "Mr. Stevie", i.e. Steve Wilson (see Exhibit C pages 54-61).

In late November, 1988 a series of telephone conversations occurred involving Janet Lossa and others that your affiant believes indicate that Lossa was anticipating a delivery of cocaine from her southern California sources, this delivery being scheduled to occur on Friday, November 25, 1988. This delivery was subsequently rescheduled for the beginning of the following week (see pages 74-77 of Exhibit C). On November 26, 1988 at approximately 10:51 a.m. Janet Lossa received a call from an unidentified male who told Lossa that he was not coming today since he had heard that the California Highway Patrol had set up check points on Interstate 5. The unidentified male told Lossa that he would come on Monday.

On November 26, 1988 at approximately 11:19 a.m. Joe DePalm called Janet Lossa and asked her if everything was "okay". Lossa told DePalm that the "guy" had called and told her he would not come until Monday. (see Exhibit C page 75)

On Monday, November 28, 1988 at approximately 1:13 p.m. FBI surveillance Agents observed a 1976 Cadillac bearing California License plate 192RFZ arrive at the residence of Janet Lossa located at 123 Appian Way, South San Francisco, California. The vehicle was driven by a Latin male (subsequently identified as Harold Londono) who was accompanied by a female passenger, both of whom were photographed by FBI

Agents. Both individuals entered Lossa's residence and shortly thereafter departed the residence and left the area in the Cadillac.

On Tuesday, November 29, 1988 at approximately 10:19 a.m. Janet Lossa was called by an unidentified male who told Lossa that he needed her help, he wanted "half". Lossa stated that that was no problem since she had "ugly ones and pretty ones". The unidentified male said he wanted a blond with blue eyes and that he would come by her house today. Your affiant believes that this conversation indicates that Lossa has now received a delivery of cocaine, some being of higher quality.

On December 4, 1988, at 12:12 p.m., Janet Lossa called Guillermo Diaz from her home and Diaz informed her "Stevie" wanted to get together. Lossa told Diaz to set up a lunch meeting for Tuesday (December 6, 1988).

On December 4, 1988, at 5:49 p.m., Guillermo Diaz called Janet Lossa at her residence. They discussed meeting the next day and Diaz asked Lossa what numbers he should give "Stevie". Lossa and Diaz agreed they may have to "share a point", but concurred that that was alright to get started. They discussed a figure "Stevie" (Steve Wilson) wanted as "12" and agreed it "had to go".

On December 5,1988, at 8:00 p.m., Guillermo Diaz called Janet Lossa at her residence and they agreed to meet the next day.

On December 6, 1988, at 12:30 p.m., Diaz called Lossa at home and reminded her of their appointment. She indicated she was leaving in 5 minutes.

On December 6, 1988, FBI Agents observed Guillermo Diaz, Janet Lossa and Steve Wilson meet at Vanessi's Restaurant, 1177 California Street, San Francisco, at approximately 1:10 p.m. The meeting lasted until about 2:35 p.m.

On December 9, 1988 FBI surveillance Agents followed Joe DePalm from Lossa's residence in South San Francisco, California to the intersection of Interstate 5 and the Pasadena Freeway, just north of Los Angeles, California. At this time DePalm exited the Interstate, turned around and proceeded to drive back to his residence at 1481 9th Street, Oakland, California. Shortly thereafter DePalm contacted Janet Lossa via telephone and told her that he had been followed. Lossa asked DePalm about the "papers" and DePalm told her that they were "okay". Lossa told DePalm to take the "car" to a specific location in the Bay Area. Immediately subsequent to this call Janet Lossa telephonically contacted Nora Kennedy and gave her instructions as to the fact someone would be coming to leave a car at her residence that contained two very important boxes. Your affiant believes that the "two very important boxes" contained Lossa's payment for the cocaine delivered to her on Monday, November 28, 1988.

On December 10, 1988 at approximately 2:40 p.m. Janet Lossa called Nora Kennedy from her place of business, The Pierrot Gift Shop, and told her to go to Anna's, Anna's being the residence of Anna Dorado, 414 Holyoke Avenue, San Francisco, California. At 3:30 p.m. that same day Nora Kennedy contacted

Janet Lossa at The Pierrot Gift Shop indicating that she had arrived at the Holyoke residence, but Anna was not home. Janet advised her that Anna would be there shortly. At approximately 3:46 p.m. FBI surveillance Agents observed the previously referenced (see page 8) 1976 Cadillac, California License 192RFZ arrive at the Holyoke residence, and they further observed Anna Dorodo motion the Cadillac into the garage. The surveilling Agents then observed the garage door being pulled down after the Cadillac had entered. At approximately 4:13 p.m. the surveilling Agents observed the Cadillac depart the Holyoke residence. Shortly thereafter FBI Agents stopped the Cadillac and subsequently arrested Harold Londono and Maritza A. Linares. Agents subsequently determined that Londono and Linares were identical to the persons photgraphed on November 28, 1988, incident to their visit to Lossa's South San Francisco residence. The arresting Agents subsequently determined that hidden under the rear seat was a beige plastic shopping bag containing $124,026.00 U.S. Currency. Your affiant believes that this money was Lossa's payment for the November 28, 1988 cocaine delivery that DePalm failed to deliver on December 9, 1988 to Lossa's "Los Angeles" suppliers.

Coincident to the arrest of several subjects in this case, a number of search warrants were executed at the residences of the subjects. Your affiant has reviewed the search warrant inventories written by the searching Agents and the following list reflects certain items of evidentiary value that were seized:

On December 12, 1988 the following evidence was seized at 650 Trestle Glen, Oakland, California, the residence of Stephen Wilson and Denise Smith: #1 "Brandt" Money Counting Machine, #2 Numerous financial records, bank statements and account records for Stephen Wilson and Denise Smith, #3 Income tax returns for Stephen Wilson, #4 $276,837.00 U.S. Currency ($50,887.00 being found in the residence, and $225,950.00 being found in paper bags in the trunk of a vehicle registered to Denise E. Smith which was parked in the garage of the residence), #5 pagers, #6 receipts and billings for construction, renovation and furnishings for defendant property, 5645 Bacon Road, Oakland, CA.

On December 11, 1988 the following evidence was seized at 66 Red Hill Circle, Tiburon, California, the residence of Guillermo Diaz and Kathleen Richmond: #1 narcotics paraphernalia, #2 .4 grams of cocaine packaged in a Mexican Peso note, #3 Cocaine residue on three items seized, #4 a mixture of cocaine and marijuana totaling 2.4 grams.

On December 12, 1988 the following evidence was seized at 123 Appian Way, South San Francisco, California, the residence of Janet Lossa: #1 Ohaus Triple Beam Scale, #2 plastic bag and a shoe box containing cocaine residue, #3 empty packages believed to be kilogram packaging containing cocaine residue, #4 three packages containing a total of 680 grams of cocaine (i.e. #1 113.09g total -97g net -86%; #2 431.01g total -368g net -85%; #3 215.38g total -215g net -85%).

On December 13, 1988 the following evidence was seized

at 619 Manzinita, Corte Madera, California, the residence of Jan

Hightower: #1 Digital pagers, #2 police scanner, #3 cocaine

handbook. The following evidence was seized from the storage

locker of Jan Hightower located at the storage house at 1325

East Francisco Boulevard, San Rafael, California, storage bin

A10: #1 two boxes containing 1668 grams of cocaine which were

wrapped in Christmas paper in a Macy's Department store shopping

bag found in a Duraflame box (i.e. #1 984.68g total -798g net

-81%; #2 995.09g total -870g net -87%).

On December 13, 1988 the search of a 1976 Cadillac,

California License 192RFZ driven by Harold Londono: #1

$124,000.00 in U.S. Currency. This search and seizure was

coincident to the arrest of the driver of the Cadillac, Harold

Londono.

Interviews of various persons have been conducted by

agents involved in this case investigation and the results of

these interviews have been related to your affiant. The persons

interviewed have stated the following based upon their personal

dealings with Steve Wilson. Wilson was receiving from one

individual kilograms of cocaine from late 1985 until the summer

of 1986 for a total of approximately 13 kilograms. One ten kilo

transaction occurred at 650 Trestle Glen, Oakland, California

for which Wilson paid $300,000.00. From mid-1988 until December

1988, Wilson spoke and met with two persons who disclosed that

they discussed supplying Wilson with multi-kilo quantities of

cocaine. Details of the discussions included the price per

kilo, the manner of payment, and the schedule of delivery. The ultimate consummation of the drug sale was interrupted by the December 1988 FBI execution of arrest and search warrants.

Shortly after the execution of the search warrant on Steve Wilson's residence at 650 Trestle Glen, Oakland, California, Steve Wilson moved out and placed the property on the market for sale. Within the year, the property sold.

"SOURCE AND APPLICATION OF FUNDS" AND FINANCIAL ANALYSIS

This portion of the affidavit includes a "Source and Application of Funds" computation regarding the known sources of funds and expenditures for the years 1986 through 1988 for Stephen Wilson and Denise Smith. The "Source and Application of Funds" computation was completed by Richard A. Nossen (see Exhibit D).

Richard A. Nossen was a former employee of the United States Internal Revenue Service from 1950 through 1974 and during that period held the following positions: Special Agent, Group Manager, Chief of the Technical Training Division, Staff Assistant to the Director of the Intelligence Division, and Assistant Director of the Intelligence Division. Since Mr. Nossen's retirement from the Internal Revenue Service in December, 1974 he has served as an instructor at law enforcement training academies throughout the United States and Canada; as a consultant to criminal investigators and prosecutors throughout the United States and Canada; and he has served as an expert witness in all aspects of financial crimes relating to "White

Collar" investigations, political corruption investigations and in various types of racketeering cases, including major narcotics cases.

Mr. Nossen has qualified as an expert witness in U.S. District Court, in San Francisco, California, Richmond, Virginia and Tampa, Florida. Mr. Nossen has also qualified as an expert witness in numerous states courts including New York, Virginia, North Carolina, Georgia and California.

Mr. Nossen has developed over these years a series of investigative techniques, the primary objectives of these techniques being the ability to trace the hidden ownership of assets, the development of evidence for "net worth" analysis, and in the preparation of statements of "Source and Application of Funds".

Mr. Nossen over the years has examined the federal and state income tax returns of hundreds of individuals who have been subjects of criminal case matters relating to violations of both federal and state narcotics laws.

Since December, 1989 to the present Mr. Nossen has been involved in the examination of voluminous bank and other financial records of Stephen Wilson and Denise E. Smith. The evidence gathered (including evidence taken in the search of 650 Trestle Glen, Oakland) during the course of this analysis by Mr. Nossen of the Wilson and Smith financial matters for years 1986 through 1988 has clearly indicated that Wilson and Smith have co-mingled their funds, and that they frequently were involved in financial transactions, expenditures, bank account activity, and the like, acting in a joint or common manner. This evidence coupled with the fact that the case investigation has indicated that Smith is Wilson's paramour, and that they were living together during this period, justifies the preparation of a combined "Source and Application of Funds" computation.

Mr. Nossen has advised your affiant that based on his examination, coupled with his experience in these matters, Mr. Nossen has made the following conclusion (see Exhibit D):

#1 During the years 1986-1988 Stephen Wilson and Denise E. Smith have collectively expended $1,217,196.72.

#2 During the same three year period they disclosed total source of funds of $546,939.06.

#3 Total expenditures in <u>excess</u> of "known" sources of funds for Stephen Wilson and Denise Smith total $670,257.66.

Mr. Nossen has advised your affiant that the "known" source of funds figure is comprised of the total amount of income disclosed in the income tax returns of Mr. Wilson during the years 1986 through 1988, and the other source of funds disclosed on Exhibit D. Mr. Nossen has noted, however, that the income disclosed in the Stephen Wilson income tax returns for the years in question is <u>not</u> identified as to its source i.e. the returns only reflecting it to be "miscellaneous" income. Mr. Nossen has advised your affiant that based on his experience this is the typical modus operandi of drug traffickers, and other types of racketeers who are attempting to conceal from the government the fact that they are engaged in some type of illegal activity for monetary gain.

Mr. Nossen has advised your affiant that the 1988 income tax return of Denise E. Smith disclosed "other" income of $20,000.00. Once again the source of this income is not identified. This 1988 income tax return of Ms. Smith was filed after Ms. Smith and Mr. Wilson became aware of the fact that an investigation was being conducted of their activities by the federal government. Mr. Nossen has advised your affiant that the failure of Ms. Smith to disclose the source of her income is again indicative of the conduct of a person who is attempting to conceal the fact that part, or all of their expenditures are being made with funds stemming from illegal sources of income.

Mr. Nossen has advised your affiant that the majority of the deposits made into the separate and joint accounts of Stephen Wilson and Denise Smith was in the form of cash. It is the opinion of your affiant, knowledgeable IRS Agents with whom your affiant has worked, and Mr. Nossen, that the business of narcotics trafficking is cash intensive, if not cash exclusive.

Mr. Nossen has advised your affiant that the total amount of expenditures that have been included in his "Source and Application of Funds" analysis does <u>not</u> include all of Wilson's and Smith's living expenses, e.g. food, medical, clothing. The "Source and Application of Funds" computation includes only those expenditures that were made through their checking accounts, and a few specific cash expenditures that have been documented through records seized from their residence, or that have been documented through interviews of third party vendors. Mr. Nossen has advised your affiant that if Wilson and Smith's living expenses were included in the computation, a significant increase in the total amount of their expenditures in excess of their "legitimate" sources of funds would result.

In determining that Wilson and Smith's expenditures are far in excess of their disclosed and known sources of funds, Mr. Nossen has advised that Wilson and Smith must necessarily had other source(s) of funds available to them during the years in question. Based on his analysis, Mr. Nossen has concluded that these funds were from, or were derived from illegitimate sources.

Your affiant has been advised by Special Agents of the Internal Revenue Service (IRS), James Skeldon and Thomas Lupori that on October 29, 1990 they interviewed Felix Stuckey and Frederick L. Sleet regarding their involvement in the preparation of Stephen Wilson's 1988 federal income tax return. IRS Agents Skeldon and Lupori have advised your affiant that Stephen Wilson's 1987 Federal Income Tax return reflected approximately $67,000.00 in "miscellaneous" income, and that his 1988 return disclosed approximately $219,000.00 in "miscellaneous" income. Agents Skeldon and Lupori noted that this marked increase in declared "miscellaneous" income on the part of Wilson occurred subsequent to a Federal search warrant being executed at Wilson's residence at 650 Trestle Glen, Oakland, California on December 12, 1988, during which Federal Agents seized $276,837.00 in U.S. Currency; $50,887.00 were found in the residence, and $225,950.00 were found in paper bags in the trunk of a vehicle registered to Denise E. Smith which was parked in the garage of the residence. On May 30, 1989 Wilson with the assistance of Felix Stuckey filed a claim for a portion of the seized currency, i.e. the $50,887.00 seized from the residence. During the course of the October 29, 1990 interview Mr. Sleet stated that he was not informed of the existence of this cash while preparing Wilson's 1988 tax return. Mr. Sleet stated that he had been informed about the $225,950.00 U.S. Currency found in the trunk of Smith's car, but was told none of this money was Smith's or Wilson's.

When asked by the IRS agents as to the source of Mr. Wilson's income, Mr. Sleet stated that he did not know the source of Mr. Wilson's income. Mr. Sleet went on to state that Wilson has "various" occupations and is "just around making money", or words to that effect.

Your affiant has been advised by Special Agents of the IRS that interviews have been conducted with Stephen Wilson's mother, Gloria Blackburn, his father, Lionel Wilson, and his brother, Lionel Wilson, Junior. In all instances the interviewees stated that they had never given Stephen Wilson any significant amount of money during the period 1986-1988.

Your affiant has been advised by Special Agents of the IRS and FBI that an interview was conducted on February 15, 1991 of Robin Wilson (Stephen Wilson's brother). During the interview Robin Wilson stated that on 10/31/86 he loaned Stephen Wilson $24,000.00 as part of a real estate transaction. Robin Wilson stated that he gave his brother the loan in the form of a cashier's check, and that Stephen Wilson repaid the loan in a series of cash payments during the next 12-18 months.

Investigation has failed to reveal any significant income being derived from legitimate employment by Stephen Wilson for the years 1986 to the present.

Based on the above facts and circumstances, there is probable cause to believe that Stephen Wilson purchased the residence located at 5645 Bacon Road, Oakland, California with proceeds derived from illegal narcotics transactions and used said residence to facilitate the distribution of controlled substances, to wit cocaine, a felony under Title 21, United States Code. The property located at 5645 Bacon Road, Oakland, California is located in the Northern District of California, and is subject to seizure and forfeiture pursuant to Title 21, United States Code, Sections 881(a)(6) and (7).

STEPHEN R. DYBSKY
Special Agent
Federal Bureau of Investigation

SUBSCRIBED and SWORN to before me
this _____ day of _________, 1991.

UNITED STATES DISTRICT COURT JUDGE

STEVE WILSON AND DENISE SMITH
COMBINED SOURCE AND APPLICATION OF FUNDS
1986-1988

| | 1986 | | 1987 | | 1988 | | 1986-1988 WILSON-SMITH | |
	WILSON	SMITH	WILSON	SMITH	WILSON	SMITH	TOTALS	DESCRIPTION OF EVIDENCE
SOURCES OF FUNDS:								
ADJUSTED GROSS INCOME	85,720.00	29,283.97	66,272.00	35,548.30	219,442.00	56,603.00	492,869.27	TAX RETURNS
1986 FEDERAL INCOME TAX REFUND			123.00	2,524.39			2,647.39	TAX RETURNS
1987 FEDERAL INCOME TAX REFUND						2,853.00	2,853.00	TAX RETURNS
1986 STATE INCOME TAX REFUND				784.66			784.66	TAX RETURNS
REFUND ON PURCHASE OF 1988 ACURA						1,651.90	1,651.90	OAKLAND ACURA REMITTANCE
PROCEEDS OF LOAN FROM PAM JACOBSEN						15,000.00	15,000.00	PROMISSORY NOTE
PROCEEDS OF CREDIT UNION LOAN #12940				4,800.00			4,800.00	LOAN APPLICATION
REFUND ON PURCH. OF BURNHAM CT. PROP.						282.84	282.84	LETTER AND CKECK
LAKESIDE DRIVE RENTAL INCOME						7,650.00	7,650.00	COPY OF LEASE
WITHDRAWALS FROM BA SVGS #0296-6-00755						18,400.00	18,400.00	TRANSCRIPT OF ACCOUNT
TOTAL SOURCES OF FUNDS	85,720.00	29,283.97	66,395.00	43,657.35	219,442.00	102,440.74	546,939.06	
EXPENDITURES:								
ESTIMATED TAX PAYMENTS	28,000.00		20,123.00		32,000.00		80,123.00	SCHEDULES - TAX RETURNS
WITHHOLDING TAXES		5,643.39		6,162.00		7,069.00	18,874.39	SCHEDULES - TAX RETURNS
PMTS BK OF OAKLAND(ORIG.LOAN APR 1983)			24,196.21		50,000.00		74,196.21	LOAN DOC.BANK OF OAKLAND.
DOWN PAYM.#1 D. BURNHAM, CRT 803,S.F.						65,169.90	65,169.90	CLSG.STMT. CHICAGO TITLE CO.
DOWN PAYMENT ON 1988 ACURA						11,300.00	11,300.00	GFACO CR.UN. LOAN DOCUMENTS.
PAYMENT OF LOAN FROM PAM JACOBSEN						15,000.00	15,000.00	BANK OF AM.CC#0008318321.
DOWN PAYMENT ON 5645 BACON ROAD	66,120.00						66,120.00	
PROP. TAXES ON 5645 BACON ROAD (87-88)			2,578.52		3,298.91		5,877.43	MONEY ORDER,C.C.,TAX BILL.
MORTGAGE PYMTS BACON RD PROP			24,883.55		29,090.15		53,973.70	TRANSCRIPT OF PAYMENTS
KNOWN CURRENCY EXPENDITURES	2,811.69		13,261.86	15,631.42	11,760.67	8,846.00	52,311.64	SCHEDULE ATTACHED.
DEPOSITS TO BA SVGS #0294-6-00755						11,051.92	11,051.92	TRANSCRIPT OF ACCOUNT
CHECKING ACCOUNT EXPENDITURES:								
BA 04081-00418		83,212.09		75,178.14		28,331.81 (1)	186,722.04	BANK RECORDS
GW 117-805351-8			32,205.94		44,336.46 (1)		76,542.40	BANK RECORDS
GW 117-804966-4	52,311.12		12,842.68				65,153.80	BANK RECORDS
SP 823-043-831 (TROUSDALE)			5,656.90		15,614.36		21,271.26	BANK RECORDS
CB 0221032675 (TROUSDALE)	91,393.72		21,885.46		23,392.85 (2)		136,672.03	BANK RECORDS
CASH SEIZURE - WILSON RESIDENCE						50,887.00	50,887.00	FBI AGENTS
CASH SEIZURE - WILSON GARAGE						225,950.00	225,950.00	FBI AGENTS
TOTAL EXPENDITURES	240,636.53	88,855.48	157,634.12	96,971.56	486,330.40	146,768.63	1,217,196.72	
EXPENDITURES IN EXCESS OF KNOWN SOURCES OF INCOME	154,916.53	59,571.51	91,239.12	53,314.21	266,888.40	44,327.89	670,257.66	

(1) DOES NOT INCLUDE INCLUDE DOWNPAYMENT ON BURNHAM COURT ($28,169;$36,000;$1,000) NOR DOWNPAYMENT ON ACURA ($10,000).
(2) DOES NOT INCLUDE $26,500 OF ESTIMATED TAXES NOR $50,000 OF LOAN PAYMENTS TO BANK OF OAKLAND SHOWN ABOVE.

BY DEANNE FITZMAURICE/THE CHRONICLE

A marshal walked past the pool of Stephen Wilson's Oakland mansion, which was seized by agents

Home of Ex-Mayor's Son Seized

Oakland mansion was purchased with drug money, FBI claims

By Jim Doyle
Chronicle Staff Writer

Federal agents have seized an Oakland mansion belonging to Stephen Wilson, who is a suspect in a cocaine-trafficking investigation. Wilson is a son of Oakland's former mayor.

There is probable cause to believe that Stephen Wilson purchased the home with "proceeds derived from illegal narcotics transactions" and that he used it to arrange cocaine deals, according to an affidavit filed yesterday in U.S. District Court by FBI Special Agent Stephen R. Dybsky.

The FBI has suspected Wilson, 44, the youngest son of former Mayor Lionel Wilson, as being part of a cocaine distribution network since 1988, but no charges have been filed against him.

FBI agents and U.S. marshals seized Wilson's home at 5645 Bacon Road in the Oakland hills Tuesday. They found only a few home furnishings but "some evidence of habitation," said Assistant U.S. Attorney Lizabeth A. McKibben, who is with the organized crime strike force.

She would not comment on Wilson's whereabouts except to say that no arrest warrant has been issued for him.

Wilson could not be reached for comment.

Nearly $300,000 in cash seized during a 1988 raid at Wilson's former residence is also the subject of a civil complaint filed by the government, McKibben said. Under the law, anyone who claims to have an interest in the seized property may contest the forfeiture in U.S. District Court.

Wilson's five-bedroom home, located on a private lane near Skyline Drive, is valued at $1 million. It has a swimming pool and an elaborate security system including huge, wrought-iron fences.

Wilson purchased the home through a friend in 1986 for $705,000, and spent several thousand dollars refurbishing it, the affidavit said. The most recently listed owner of the property was Trousdale Investments, a business name used by Wilson.

The front gate was chained and padlocked yesterday. A sign read: "Property of the U.S. Government."

Feds seize land of Lionel Wilson's son

By Seth Rosenfeld
OF THE EXAMINER STAFF

Federal agents have seized another Oakland property allegedly belonging to the youngest son of former Oakland Mayor Lionel Wilson, claiming he bought it with money from years of dealing cocaine, heroin and other drugs.

An FBI affidavit, filed in support of the seizure and unsealed Thursday in U.S. District Court in San Francisco, revealed a new FBI money laundering probe of Steve Wilson and an alleged associate who works as a drug counselor.

It disclosed new allegations that for nearly two decades Wilson has been a large volume drug dealer and an armed robber.

"He has been under investigation by federal authorities since 1988 for large-scale narcotics trafficking in the Bay Area, money laundering, and tax evasion," FBI agent Randy Scott said in the affidavit.

Based on the testimony, Magistrate William Garrett, in an order also unsealed Thursday, authorized the seizure of a valuable vacant lot at 3911 to 3921 Cerrito Ave. He ruled there was "probable cause" that Wilson bought the lot — valued at between $500,000 and $700,000 — with drug money, and then arranged a series of sham real estate deals in an attempt to hide his ownership.

Wilson, 45, never has been charged with any drug crime and

he has denied dealing drugs. He and his lawyer could not be reached for comment.

The seizure showed that law enforcement officials are continuing to target him for alleged drug dealing. Last year, they seized a posh Oakland hills home from Wilson on grounds it was bought with drug money.

Ironically, the affidavit alleges that much of the drug dealing occurred between 1978 and 1991, the years his father, as mayor of Oakland, struggled to overcome that city's mounting drug problems.

The affidavit alleges that:

▶ As early as 1976, Los Angeles police linked Steve Wilson to heroin dealing when they stopped him in a Mercedes-Benz and found a quarter-pound of heroin in his passenger's possession. Wilson said he owned the car, but claimed to be an unemployed laborer.

▶ In the late 1970s, a drug suspect told Oakland police that Wilson was his supplier, and other suspects and prostitutes claimed Wilson was involved in armed robberies of other drug dealers.

▶ In 1979 and 1980, said Oakland Police Capt. Larry Rodrigue, "it was common knowledge" in the department's narcotics unit that Wilson was a cocaine dealer; "however, no formal investigation was ever begun." The affidavit does not say why.

▶ Between 1986 and 1988, Wilson and his paramour Denise Smith listed income of $546,939.

But during the same period they actually spent $1.2 million, or some $668,000 more than they reported earning, the affidavit said. Wilson did not identity any income source on his tax returns other than "miscellaneous" income.

▶ In May 1992, convicted drug dealer Willie Kichen Jr. alleged that Wilson sold pot, cocaine, heroin and methamphetamine, and between the mid-1970s and 1981 Wilson's alleged drug profits seemed to increase "steadily."

▶ In 1988, FBI agents determined that Wilson was a "participant" in a large-scale cocaine ring allegedly based in North Beach, with ties to the East Coast's Gambino Mafia family.

▶ In December 1988, FBI agents searched Wilson's Oakland home on Trestle Glen Road and seized $225,950 in cash and a money counter.

The affidavit also alleges that Wilson bought the Cerrito Avenue property in 1980 for $350,000, and in 1991 sold it to his girlfriend's mother for $52,313. Just three months later, it said, she in turn sold the property for $150,000 to Raymond McMurray, whom an informant identified as Wilson's "flunkie" and assistant in hiding Wilson's ownership.

McMurray, who has worked 13 years as a counselor at HAART, a private methadone clinic in San Leandro, told FBI agents he learned of the property from a newspaper ad, the affidavit said.

McMurray, in an interview Monday, denied any role in drug dealing or money laundering. He said he had purchased various properties legitimately with help from other investors and proceeds from other property sales and second mortgages.

BAY AREA

Home of son of ex-Oakland mayor seized

Associated Press

OAKLAND   Federal agents have seized the hillside home of Stephen Wilson, son of former Oakland Mayor Lionel Wilson, saying they believe he bought it with the proceeds from narcotics sales.

However, Stephen Wilson, who was first described by the FBI in 1988 as linked to a cocaine ring, has not been charged with any crime.

The $700,000 home was confiscated Tuesday with a warrant issued by U.S. Magistrate Joan Brennan, who found probable cause to believe it was bought with illicit drug money. To recover the home, Wilson would have to show that it was not bought with drug proceeds or used for drug dealing.

Wilson, youngest son of the former mayor, is a former Oakland high school football star who was partially paralyzed in a 1971 shooting.

Attorney G. William Hunter said he got a call from Wilson on Wednesday and expects to represent him in a challenge to the seizure of his house.

Hunter declined comment on FBI allegations of drug-dealing, saying he had not seen the statements. But he said, "I think that's probably indicative of their case, making those representations or accusations and they haven't charged him."

Lionel Wilson was defeated for re-election as mayor last year and is now a Walnut Creek attorney and an Oakland port commissioner. He has not been accused of any wrongdoing but was interviewed, along with other relatives, by tax agents trying to determine where Stephen Wilson got large sums of money, the FBI said.

The FBI said it searched another of Stephen Wilson's Oakland homes in December 1988 and found $50,000 in cash, and another $225,000 in a car in the garage; the car is owned by Wilson's lover. No drugs were seized. Wilson, who was present during the search, was not arrested.

In the most extensive public declaration to date of Wilson's alleged

MORE STATE NEWS

Los Angeles police chief says he won't resign.   **3D**

activities, FBI Agent Stephen Dybsky said in a court affidavit last week that the ex-mayor's son was "a participant in (a) cocaine distribution conspiracy" that has been under investigation since early 1987.

The first indication of Wilson's involvement came in a wiretapped telephone call in May 1988 from Wilson to another participant, Guillermo Diaz, one of many such calls, Dybsky said. Diaz and three other people were arrested in December 1988, pleaded guilty to cocaine charges and were sentenced to prison, the agent said.

Dybsky said the arrests interrupted a planned sale of "multi-kilo quantities of cocaine" to Wilson that had been negotiated by two unnamed people since mid-1988.

To Corroborate Evidence of Drug Trafficking by a Street Gang (R Street Crew Case)

On July 2, 1992, a United States District Court jury convicted five defendants on multiple felony counts, ranging from operating a criminal enterprise, murder, drug conspiracy, and other related charges. The trial lasted for more than four months and the jury deliberated for 10 days before bringing in their verdict. The prosecution team included AUSA's Russell Duncan, Jeffrey Ragsdale, and Odessa Vincent.

Various witnesses testified concerning the defendants' lavish spending sprees on Rodeo Drive in Beverly Hills. The defendants must forfeit two houses, more than a dozen luxury cars, a 4-wheel drive truck, and a significant amount of cash.

During the course of trial preparation AUSA Odessa Vincent contacted the authors to request an analysis of an array of financial records in an attempt to determine the extent of the expenditures of two of the defendants who had nominal sources of legitimate income. The records were obtained during the course of the investigation by FBI Special Agent Gregory Scott and Detective Guy Poirer, Washington, D.C. Metropolitan Police Department.

During the course of the trial FBI Supervisory Special Agent Elliott Leary testified concerning the nature of the expenditures which led to the introduction into evidence of appropriate source and application of funds schedules.

The following schedule is similar to the schedule introduced into evidence to strengthen the overall case against two of the principal defendants. Additional facts of the case are covered in newspaper articles which follow.

```
                    MICHAEL AND JOYCE BOYD
                    SOURCE AND APPLICATION OF FUNDS
                    1987-1988
                                                    1987-1988
                                   1987      1988    TOTAL    DESCRIPTION
                                   ----      ----    ----     ---------- ---------- ----------
SOURCES OF FUNDS:
1987 Adjusted Gross Income       12992.19                    1987 Tax Return
1988 Earnings of Mr. Boyd                  15213.79          Army 1987 W-2
1986 Tax Refund                    559.16                    Cancelled IRS check
1987 Tax Refund                              856.00          1987 Tax Return
Interest-Pentagon Credit Union     211.41    252.80          Credit Union statements
Interest Bethesda Hills                       48.00          1988 1099-INT Form
Insurance Settlement              1706.10                    Hartford Co. cancelled check
                                ---------  ---------  ---------
TOTAL SOURCES OF FUNDS          15468.86   16370.59   31839.45
                                ---------  ---------  ---------
EXPENDITURES:
1988 Mercedes 560 SEL:
    Cash in Advance                        39000.00          Contract,Canc. ck,bank record
    Aug.-Nov. Payments                      4062.98          Reciept
Purchase of Hair Salon                     35000.00          Cashier Ck,CTR,Purchase Agree
Bethesda  Hills Rent Payments      975.00                    Money Order Receipts
Credit Union Loan Payments        3912.15   4267.80          Credit Union Statements
Withdrawals Credit Union          1900.00   7350.00          Credit Union Statements
Ck. Withdrawls-Perpetual #00798470 2738.08                   Bank statements, checks
Ck. Withdrawls-Perpetual #880-3748-6 3313.00 14162.00        Bank statements
Ck. Withdrawls-Independence #0199-12450 14437.40 18867.30    Bank statements, checks
                                ---------  ---------  ---------
TOTAL EXPENDITURES              27275.63  122710.08  149985.71
                                ---------  ---------  ---------
EXPENDITURES IN EXCESS OF
REPORTED INCOME                 -11806.77 -106339.49 -118146.26
                                ========= ========= =========
```

WEDNESDAY, JULY 22, 1992

The Washington Post

5 Convicted In R Street Drug Trial

Racketeering Law Used to Prosecute D.C. Gang Leaders

By Michael York
Washington Post Staff Writer

A U.S. District Court jury yesterday convicted three men of operating a criminal enterprise that used murder and intimidation to control drug sales in a Northeast Washington neighborhood.

Two other defendants, who prosecutors said also were members of the R Street Crew, were convicted of drug conspiracy and other charges.

The case, which took five months to try, has been watched by federal prosecutors and defense lawyers across the country because it was one of a few attempts, and the first in the District, to use sophisticated anti-racketeering laws against a suspected street drug gang.

Although the jurors acquitted all defendants of racketeering, defense lawyers said the prosecutors' strategy of using the law made it easier to include other crimes, such as murder, in the case and thus made their defense problems far more complex. As a practical matter, the racketeering acquittals had little effect because the jury voted to convict on the more serious offense of operating a continuing criminal enterprise.

"Today's verdict is a tremendous victory for the people of the District of Columbia," said U.S. Attorney Jay B. Stephens. "It demonstrates our unrelenting commitment to use the full arsenal of laws available to us to bring to justice drug kingpins who are responsible for much of the human devastation affecting this community."

From the start of the trial, prosecutors portrayed the R Street defendants as high-rolling drug dealers who built an organization complete with enforcers, drug processors, distributors, lieutenants and street runners. The organization operated between 1983 and 1991, conducting much of its business near the corner of Lincoln Road and R Street NE.

Various witnesses described lavish spending sprees on Rodeo Drive in Beverly Hills, Calif., high-speed chases in Mercedes-Benz sedans

See TRIAL, A7, Col. 1

TRIAL, From A1

and an unsuccessful drive-by shooting attack on convicted drug kingpin Rayful Edmond III.

In addition to the continuing criminal enterprise counts, an offense that carries a mandatory sentence of life without parole, Kevin F. Williams-Davis, 28, Anthony T. Nugent, 27, and Darryl D. Williams, 24, were convicted of second-degree murder. Williams-Davis and Nugent also were convicted of six counts of assault with a deadly weapon. Prosecutors said the killings were committed to bolster the drug operation.

Alba D. Restrepo, 46, and Joyce Boyd, 39, were convicted of conspiring to distribute drugs and other drug offenses. Those convictions carry mandatory minimum sentences of 10 years, although federal sentencing guidelines could provide for minimum terms of at least 30 years.

Nineteen other suspected gang members have yet to be tried.

The jury announced its verdict after 10 days of deliberations. Merely reading the 28-page verdict took more than 30 minutes. Afterward, U.S. District Judge George Revercomb ordered the jurors to return tomorrow to decide whether the defendants must forfeit two houses, more than a dozen luxury cars and four-wheel-drive trucks and more than $60,000 in cash and bank deposits.

Outside the courthouse, Kenneth M. Robinson, who defended Nugent, seized on the racketeering acquittals to declare that "the jury concluded there was no R Street Crew, but that there have been incidents of drug dealing for a number of years."

The law, known as RICO for the Racketeering Influenced Corrupt Organizations Act, was designed as a tool to fight traditional organized crime, but it has been used in public corruption cases as well as against drug gangs. To win a conviction under the law, prosecutors must prove that the defendants operated an "enterprise" and that they committed at least two designated crimes, or "racketeering acts" as part of the enterprise. The continuing criminal enterprise charge, of which the three gang leaders were convicted, required proof that each defendant supervised at least five subordinates in the illegal organization.

As the jury's foreman, Janet Farley, read the verdicts, Boyd collapsed in tears in a seat behind the defense table. Later, Revercomb denied a request that she be allowed to remain free on bond, agreeing with Assistant U.S. Attorney Odessa Vincent that, because Boyd faces the possibility of a 30-year sentence, there is a risk she might flee.

Williams-Davis, Nugent and Darryl Williams, dressed in colorful, flowing Nigerian shirts, sat impassively as the verdicts were announced. Restrepo appeared to weep quietly as an interpreter whispered the verdicts in her ear.

Afterward, lawyers for each of the three gang leaders asked that the men be transferred to Lorton prison from the D.C. jail, where they have been confined since their arrests.

Leonard Birdsong, who defended Williams-Davis, said his client wanted to be moved because Williams-Davis is a devoutly religious Muslim who has been disturbed by the noise and the sometimes raucous environment at the jail.

"He's a very spiritual person," Birdsong said. "He likes to pray, and it's not a very spiritual place."

Revercomb said he would ask that the defendants be moved to Lorton after the jury decides on the forfeitures. The judge scheduled sentencing hearings for October, after which they will be sent to federal prisons.

The assault charges and one of the murder charges against Williams-Davis and Nugent stemmed from a shooting that prosecutors said was a climax of the gang's violence.

That last battle, at midday on April 18, 1989, at an auto repair shop in Northeast Washington, left one man dead and another shot 10 times. Prosecutors said the three R Street leaders went to the garage to avenge the murder the previous day of Nugent's younger brother, Sean Martin, who also worked in the drug organization.

Martin was slain, prosecutors said, in retaliation for the killing a week earlier of Gerard Bailey, a rival R Street drug dealer.

Freddie Lee Bailey, Gerard Bailey's older brother, testified about being shot at the garage.

As he stood in front of the garage, Bailey said, he saw a man, his face partially hidden by a cap and sunglasses, walk across 14th Street NE toward him. When the man was about 30 feet away, Bailey said, the man raised his head, at the same time pulling a gun from his belt and starting to fire. Bailey testified that he recognized the shooter as Nugent from R Street NE, where Bailey lived with his girlfriend.

Not knowing he had already been hit by rounds from the .45-caliber pistol, Bailey turned and ran into the body shop's office where Bailey had his own gun hidden under the cushion of a couch. "I didn't make it to the gun," Bailey testified.

Another man in the garage, Francis Scrivner, died of a single bullet wound in the abdomen.

The three gang leaders had been charged with first-degree murder, but the jury convicted them of second-degree.

The Washington Post, July 23, 1992

Fear Said To Affect R St. Jury

Concerns Revealed As Panel Ends Work

By Michael York and Linda Wheeler
Washington Post Staff Writers

Several jurors in the trial of a D.C. drug gang known as the R Street Crew said yesterday they believe the verdict was partially influenced by fear of retaliation.

They also said that some jurors refused to convict on two racketeering counts because they believed—incorrectly—that those charges carried the heaviest penalties.

The seven jurors who held out for acquittal on the racketeering charges against the alleged members of the R Street Crew "were just plain scared for their personal safety," said Janet Jellison, the jury foreman. "It would have been better if we didn't have to deal with that. It was just too much."

Jellison, who said she believed the defendants were guilty of racketeering, did not elaborate on why she thought the other jurors were afraid.

Two of the six jurors interviewed said that fear of retaliation affected deliberations but that they were not fearful themselves. Two jurors said that there were concerns about safety but that they were unsure whether those fears had an impact on the jurors' votes. The other two jurors interviewed declined to discuss the safety concerns of the jury.

After a five-month trial and more than two weeks of deliberations, the jury completed its work yesterday. The jurors decided that the defendants should forfeit four luxury cars, a four-wheel drive truck, a house and $11,415 in cash as proceeds of an illegal drug operation.

On Tuesday, the jury had acquitted the five defendants of racketeering but convicted three of them of directing a drug organization and of using murder and violent assault to keep their drug conspiracy in place. The jury convicted the two other defendants on drug conspiracy charges.

Ironically, the racketeering acquittals made no difference in the pro-spective penalties. Three defendants, Kevin F. Williams-Davis, 28, Anthony T. Nugent, 27, and Darryl D. Williams, 24, were convicted of operating a continuing criminal enterprise, an offense that carries a mandatory sentence of life without parole.

Two other defendants, Alba D. Restrepo, 46, and Joyce Boyd, 39, were convicted of conspiring to distribute drugs and other drug offenses. Those convictions carry mandatory minimum sentences of 10 years, although federal sentencing guidelines could provide for minimum terms of at least 30 years.

Jellison, 35, said the jurors were deadlocked 7 to 5 for acquittal on the racketeering charges, brought under the Racketeer-Influenced and Corrupt Organizations Act.

Jellison and fellow juror Frank Garnett said the jury was well aware that this was the test case for using the act to prosecute street drug gangs. The law, devised as a tool to fight organized crime, has been used against other drug organizations, but this was the first case involving a street gang. A second such case, against the so-called P Street Crew, is scheduled for trial in October.

Jellison said she too was fearful when she realized the case involved an alleged gang that had been linked to several homicides, but she said she grew more comfortable as the trial moved on. Jellison said she lives in a neighborhood with drug trafficking problems, and she said her house and car have been burglarized in the past.

During the trial, Assistant U.S. Attorney Russell Duncan disclosed that threatening posters had appeared in the unit block of R Street NE, the base of the defendants' operations, and that some witnesses had received threats. There were no reports, however, of threats to jurors in the case.

The trial was conducted in Courtroom 10, which has a bulletproof glass wall separating the audience from the judge, lawyers and defendants.

Garnett, a postal employee, said he was surprised to learn that three defendants would receive life without parole. He said he, like other jurors, focused on the racketeering charges.

"We knew this was a first for Washington, D.C., and around the country," Garnett said. "I think they [the U.S. attorney's office] want to satisfy the public by bringing these street-level cases."

Although he understood that prosecution strategy, part of it disturbed him, Garnett said, because the government appeared more concerned with prosecuting the R Street defendants than their cocaine suppliers in Central America.

One alleged supplier, Restrepo, was among those convicted, but two others, Panamanian nationals Jaime and Guillermo Bynoe, once cooperated with the government and are now fugitives. Defense lawyers said during the trial that prosecutors allowed them to leave the country.

Garnett agreed: "They could have gone after them, but they let them go."

Much of the jury's 10 days of deliberations centered on the racketeering counts, and several jurors acknowledged that the sessions were heated but declined to elaborate.

Jellison said she already was familiar with federal racketeering laws, having written a paper for a course at George Washington University on the Mafia. She said that when she heard the government's evidence, she knew what was before them was a violation of the racketeering act.

"What I saw was an ongoing criminal enterprise," she said. "They might not have been Mafia . . . but I recognized it. I saw it."

To Overcome Drug Dealer's Motion For Summary Judgment For Return of Seized Property (Monroe Case)

Walker Bennett Monroe pled guilty to federal narcotics charges in 1988 and was sentenced to a lengthy prison term. At the time of his arrest DEA agents seized more than $800,000.00 in currency and several parcels of real estate valued at approximately $1,000,000.00.

Following Monroe's incarceration, his attorney filed a motion in federal court for Summary Judgment, requesting the return of the properties in question. The motion was supported by a lengthy comprehensive computation that purported to show that Walker Monroe and Linda Stuart had acquired all of the real estate in question over a nine-year period with legitimate funds and, therefore, was not subject to forfeiture.

The computations were further supported by copies of the income tax returns of Monroe and Stuart for the years 1979 through 1986. The returns allegedly documented their contention of the legitimacy of the funds used to acquire the real estate.

The income tax returns were rather complex. They reflected a variety of capital gains transactions and related business activities.

IF the transactions summarized in the Motion were accurate and IF they constituted a complete disclosure of their expenditures, their motion for the return of the seized real estate would appear to be credible.

AUSA Donald D. Clausen retained the authors to analyze the tax returns in question and other related records to determine whether or not the government could establish that their expenditures during the years 1979 through 1986 were in *excess* of their so-called legitimate sources of income.

Based on the information contained in the tax returns, augmented by additional expenditures evidence gathered by DEA Special Agent Douglas W. Hebert and Deputy U.S. Marshal David Meyer, the authors were able to show that in most, if not all, of the critical years they did *not* have sufficient legitimate funds available to acquire the real estate.

As a result of subsequent negotiations, their attorneys agreed to withdraw their motion and to forfeit more than 80% of the real estate in question in addition to the $800,000 cash. The following schedule is similar to the Source and Application of Funds schedule developed by the authors.

WALKER MONROE AND LINDA STUART
SOURCE AND APPLICATION OF FUNDS
1979–1988

	1979	1980	1981	1982	1983	1984	1985
SOURCES OF FUNDS:							
FUNDS AVAILABLE	$45,351.00	$46,566.00	$57,086.00	$59,994.00	$15,986.00	$17,948.00	$24,665.00
PROCEEDS SALE OF LAND							
NOTE PAYMENT RECEIVED							48,100.00
TOTAL SOURCES OF FUNDS	$45,351.00	$46,566.00	$57,086.00	$59,994.00	$15,986.00	$17,948.00	$72,765.00
EXPENDITURES:							
CHECKING ACCOUNT WITHDRAWALS:							
SOUTHWEST ACCT# 030304092	19,893.86	29,983.93					
FIB ACCT# 21139319			93,612.00 (g)	77,784.31 (h)	14,353.18 (i)	22,694.64	1,035.41
FIB ACCT# 124847715						4,582.91	49,053.05 (j)
FIB ACCT# 21134236		3,219.16	21,970.84				
LOT 4 LITTLE MAKAWAO	$20,000.00						
LOG PURCHASES		18,900.00	23,900.00	19,400.00			
LOTS 9 & 10 HAILEY	5,000.00	20,000.00					
WARM SPRINGS		25,000.00	32,000.00 (a)	31,053.00 (c)	28,545.00	27,314.00	10,000.00 (e)
LOT 6 COLD SPRINGS		5,000.00		15,750.00 (b)	14,750.00 (d)		
PURCHASE OF BMW							16,500.00
PURCHASE OF HORSES	4,710.00	700.00					
TRAVEL EXPENSES							
SEIZURE OF CURRENCY							
SEIZURE OF CURRENCY							
SEIZURE OF CURRENCY							
SEIZURE OF CURRENCY							
CURRENCY WITHDRAWAL							
TOTAL EXPENDITURES	$49,603.86	$102,803.09	$171,482.84	$143,987.31	$57,648.18	$54,591.55	$76,588.46
EXCESS OF EXPENDITURES OVER KNOWN SOURCES OF FUNDS	($4,252.86)	($56,237.09)	($114,396.84)	($83,993.31)	($41,662.18)	($36,643.55)	($3,823.46)

NOTE:

	1981	1982	1983	1985
WITHDRAWALS PER BANK STATEMENT SUMMARY	179,862.00	124,587.31	29,103.18	59,053.05
LESS EXPENDITURES LISTED SEPARATELY ABOVE:				
(a) ck# 125, 7/7/81, Andy Schernthanner	(32,000.00)			
(b) ck# 293, 12/30/81, Anderson Lumber		(15,750.00)		
(c) ck# 235, 7/20/82, Andy Schernthanner		(31,053.00)		
(d) ck# 329, 1/10/83, Payee unknown			(14,750.00)	
(e) ck# 203, 2/10/85, Andy Schernthanner				(10,000.00)
(f) ck# 420, 4/26/88, Andy Schernthanner				
LESS DEPOSIT FROM FIB #21334236 (6/81)	(7,000.00)			
LESS CHECKS INCLUDED AS WITHDRAWALS BUT NOT CLEARED [ck #224, #219 (twice) @ $15,750 each]	(47,250.00)			
	93,612.00 (g)	77,784.31 (h)	14,353.18 (i)	49,053.05 (j)

1986	1987	1988	TOTAL	EVIDENCE
	NOT	NOT		
$19,095.00	AVAILABLE	AVAILABLE	$286,691.00	FEDERAL TAX RETURNS (SCH. A−1, A−2)
		274,984.00	274,984.00	DECLARATION OF DAPHNE M. THRONE
			48,100.00	DECLARATION OF DAPHNE M. THRONE
$19,095.00	$0.00	$274,984.00	$609,775.00	
			$49,877.79	BANK RECORDS
11,969.55	8,715.05	115,369.80 (k)	345,533.94	BANK RECORDS
7,828.42	21,524.78	30,658.46	113,647.62	BANK RECORDS
			25,190.00	BANK RECORDS
			20,000.00	DECLARATION OF DAPHNE M. THRONE
			62,200.00	VENDOR RECORDS
			25,000.00	DECLARATION OF DAPHNE M. THRONE
5,000.00	9,000.00	11,036.25 (f)	178,948.25	DECLARATION OF DAPHNE M. THRONE
			35,500.00	DECLARATION OF DAPHNE M. THRONE
			16,500.00	DEA
			5,410.00	1980 FEDERAL TAX RETURNS
		17,379.40	17,379.40	TRAVEL AGENT RECORDS
		694,980.00	694,980.00	5/9/88 MONROE
		35,000.00	35,000.00	9/9/88 MONROE BMW TRUNK
		1,800.00	1,800.00	9/9/88 MONROE
		4,200.00	4,200.00	9/9/88 STUART
		174,136.00	174,136.00	9/9/88 STUART
$24,797.97	$39,239.83	$1,084,559.91	$1,805,303.00	
($5,702.97)	($39,239.83)	($809,575.91)	($1,195,528.00)	
		126,406.05		
		(11,036.25)		
		115,369.80 (k)		

To Aid in Establishing Probable Cause for Search Warrants (Bashara Case)

The following synopsis was provided by Detective Kelly Lane of the Tucson (Arizona) Police Department. Detective Lane and an undercover officer conducted a successful investigation that included the use of a Source and Application of Funds Schedule.

In February, 1990, Roger Bashara arrived in Tucson from Newport Beach, California. He was on a buying trip – a marijuana buying trip. He negotiated for and purchased 400 pounds of marijuana for $197,000 from the undercover DEA Agent. Roger's other mistake was bragging, during the negotiations, about how successful he had been over the years in his drug trade. In fact, he claimed to have acquired a valuable art collection, a yacht, expensive cars, and was currently building his dream home near San Diego. Roger was arrested and his buy money was seized. Several hours later he was bonded out of jail.

Within 48 hours, investigators began executing a dozen search and seizure warrants on Roger's residence, businesses, storage lockers, and bank accounts. Business records and data downloaded from his office computer established the existence of several "shell" corporations that Roger had created to launder the drug money. Banking transaction reports were collected and reviewed. The most valuable item was discovered in the search of Roger's residence.

Roger was not at home when his residence was searched. Acting upon the advice of his lawyer, Roger and his wife had taken a vacation to Palm Springs seeking relief from the stressful few hours he had spent in jail. A search team spent most of the day thoroughly searching his large ocean view home without finding anything significant. There were two cars parked in the garage – a Porsche and a Saab. The keys to the Saab were gone and the trunk was locked. The search team was clearing the scene when an officer decided to pry open the trunk. The trunk was empty except for one cardboard file box.

The box contained the smoking gun. Roger had neatly organized his financial history including: income tax returns, loan applications, employment resumes, real estate investments, telephone bills, business interests, bank statements, etc. A quick review of the contents revealed that Roger had overspent his legitimate (tax reported) income by hundreds of thousands of dollars. This information was used to support applications for seizure warrants of his assets including bank accounts, autos, furniture, San Diego property, and his home under construction.

The financial data also provided assistance in the criminal plea negotiations and in the settlement of the civil forfeiture action. Furthermore, it was presented to the sentencing judge to support the state's claim that Bashara had been involved in the illegal drug trade for a considerable period of time.

The following Source and Application of Funds schedule is similar to the schedule prepared by Detective Lane, Wendy Spaulding, and Joan Norvelle.

```
                    ROGER A. BASHARA                              SCHEDULE 1
              SOURCE AND APPLICATION OF FUNDS
                       1988-1990
```

	1988	1989	1990	EXHIBIT NO.	DESCRIPTION
SOURCES OF FUNDS:					
ADJ. GROSS INCOME PER FEDERAL RETURNS	10,679	NOT AVAIL	NOT AVAIL	1	FEDERAL TAX RETURNS
INTEREST ON HOME SAVINGS ACCT.		1,579		29	BANK RECORDS
WAGES - GRETCHEN BASHARA		4,839		30	W-2 - DELTA AIRLINES
TOTAL SOURCES OF FUNDS	10,679	N/A	N/A		
EXPENDITURES:					
LOANS FROM STOCKHL.-PERCEP. INVEST.	25,031			1	FEDERAL TAX RETURNS.
PURCHASE OF PIZZA PARLOR		10,000		2	HANDWRITTEN PURCH. AGREEMENT; ASSUME 25% OWNERSHIP
DOWN PAYM. DIKE RD. PROP. AZ.		2,503		3	ESCROW PAPERWORK
PAYM. OF NOTE ON DIKE RD. PROP. AZ.		5,148		4	PAYMENT SCHEDULE AND CASHIER'S CHECKS
LEASE PAYMS. 318 MORNING CANYON	16,000	24,000		5	LEASE AGREEMENT;SOME CASHIER'S CHECKS
DOWN PAYM. PURCHASE MORNING CANYON	5,000			6	SALES OFFER AND CANCELLED CHECK
CHECKS WRITTEN ON BANK ACCOUNT	20,294			7	SECURITY PACIFIC 2271064421
CHECKS WRITTEN ON BANK ACCOUNT	33,695	25,989		8	HOME SAVINGS 148904834-6
LOAN TO MARY BASHARA VIA JOHN BASHARA		15,000		9	LOAN AGREEMENT AND LETTER FROM COLETTE
JEEP CHEROKEE (NET AMOUNT)	4,500			10	SALES CONTRACTS-PUR. 5/88-$24,500;SOLD 9/88-$20,000
PAYM. FOR PLANT RESEARCH CORP. STOCK.		36,000		11	RECEIPT WOLTERMAN TO BASHARA;CHECK OF WOLTERMAN TO PRC
TRAVEL EXPENDITURES	2,704	4,098		12	COPIES OF AIRLINE TICKETS AND HOTEL BILLS
PURCHASE OF PORSCHE		50,000		13	INVOICES FROM EUROPEAN HIGH TECH
VEHICLE REPAIRS	2,444	9,898		14	VENDOR INVOICES
HOME FURNISHINGS	1,324	1,999		15	VENDOR INVOICES
JEWELRY AND CLOTHING		24,168		16	SALES TICKETS
PAYM. TO SOUTHERN CALIF. COLLEGE		1,850		17	CASHIER'S CHECK
MEDICAL INSURANCE		1,034		18	RECEIPT FROM INSURANCE COMPANY
PHOTOGRAPHY EXPENSES		305		19	SALES INVOICE
PAYMENT TO RICE ROOFING		6,545		20	CASHIER'S CHECK
UPLAND MORTGAGE (BANK OF AMERICA)	10,422	10,422		21	COPY OF YEAR END STATEMENT
INT./PENALTIES ON PY TAXES	1,658	1,120		22	TAX STATEMENTS AND CASHIER'S CHECKS
FORD BRONCO		7,200		23	CASHIER'S CHECK ($4,000) AND SALES TAX FORM
MEDICAL EXPENSES		3,350		24	SURGICAL COST ANALYSIS OF DR. LUHAN
PURCHASE OF STOCK/ HAYWOOD SECURITIES		15,891		25	CASHIER'S CHECK AND HAYWOOD STATEMENT
PURCHASE OF STOCK/DEAN WITTER		5,190		26	CASHIER'S CHECK AND DEAN WITTER STATEMENT
PURCHASE OF MARIJUANA			197,000	27	TUCSON POLICE DEPT. PROPERTY RECORDS
1989 FORD VAN		14,000		28	PER KELLY'S REPORT
OPEN SAVINGS ACCOUNT (HOME SAVINGS)		50,000		29	BANK RECORDS
STORAGE FEES		3,477		31	CASHIER'S CHECK - CIRKER HAYES STORAGE
TOTAL EXPENDITURES	123,072	329,187	197,000		
EXPEND. IN EXCESS OF REPORTED INCOME	(112,393)	N/A	N/A		

Appendix A

"ONE-ON-ONE" UNCORROBORATED TESTIMONY: THE DILEMMA OF PROSECUTORS, DEFENSE ATTORNEYS, AND THE COURTS IN FRAUD, WASTE AND ABUSE CASES

Richard A. Nossen

Reprinted from
THE NOTRE DAME LAW REVIEW
Volume 58, Number 5, June 1983
Copyright 1983 by University of Notre Dame

"One-on-One" Uncorroborated Testimony: The Dilemma of Prosecutors, Defense Attorneys, and the Courts in Fraud, Waste, and Abuse Cases

*Richard A. Nossen**

Prosecutors, defense attorneys and the courts are increasingly confronted with the "one-on-one" case. Particularly in the adjudication of offenses involving fraud, waste, and abuse, all participants in the judicial system are struggling with the problem of one-on-one, uncorroborated testimony.

I. The Problem

A claims to have paid off *B*. Of course, *B* denies having received illegal payments. *A's* credibility as a prosecution witness is often weakened because (1) he is facing an indictment; (2) he has already pled guilty to the crime in question and is awaiting sentence; or (3) he has already been sentenced and is hoping for a modification of sentence if he "cooperates" during *B's* trial. Seldom is there any corroborative evidence to support *A's* testimony that he paid off *B*, since such payoffs are generally made in currency. On the other hand, *B* vehemently denies having received illegal funds from *A* or anyone else. *B's* credibility is often strengthened because (1) he holds a high political office or a responsible position in private industry; (2) he has no criminal record; and (3) he produces an array of character witnesses during trial who testify favorably as to his reputation in the community, reinforcing his "cloak of innocence."

In the one-on-one situation the prosecutor must decide whether or not to present the case to a grand jury, and he is often under considerable pressure from the public and press. The defense attorney faces the hazard of defending a client who may be withholding the truth, often a fatal blow during trial. The judge, too, must wrestle with problems generated by the one-on-one dilemma,

---

* Criminal Justice Systems Consultant and former Assistant Director of the Criminal Investigation Division, U.S. Internal Revenue Service. Mr. Nossen has developed a variety of investigative accounting training materials for law enforcement organizations at all levels of government and for private industry. He also serves as a consultant to and as an expert witness for prosecutors in the trial of financial crimes. He is the author of *The Seventh Basic Investigative Technique*, a handbook designed for auditors, criminal investigators, and private industry security and investigative personnel; and *The Detection, Investigation and Prosecution of Financial Crimes*, published in May, 1982. Mr. Nossen resides at 11410 Edenberry Drive, Richmond, Virginia, 23236.

1020   THE NOTRE DAME LAW REVIEW   [June 1983]

such as ruling on motions to dismiss the case because of insufficient evidence, determining guilt or innocence in non-jury trials, or deciding on the extent of punishment after the jury has returned a questionable guilty verdict. The one-on-one dilemma is encountered at the investigative level as well as when a supervisory investigator or attorney must decide whether to commit valuable investigative resources to a lengthy investigation which may prove fruitless.

The dimensions of the one-on-one problem have grown in recent years due to the proliferation of so-called white collar financial crimes involving political corruption and fraudulent business practices. The problem has further compounded because most criminal investigators and their supervisors, as well as many prosecutors, are inhibited in the investigation and prosecution of fraud, waste, and abuse cases by their insufficient understanding of accounting fundamentals and the corresponding fear that they will be unable to interpret, analyze or explain complex financial transactions to a jury.

II. The Solution

In recent years one solution for the one-on-one problem has emerged, the highly successful use of video-tape recordings. However, there are a myriad of cases in which, for various reasons, the video-tape technique cannot be applied. One viable solution that is now being successfully applied in the prosecution of some of these one-on-one financial crime cases employs a modified version of the Internal Revenue Service (IRS) "net worth" technique.

For over fifty years the IRS has used a net worth computation to satisfy one of the elements of proof necessary to obtain a conviction for income tax evasion. The computation primarily determines the extent to which a taxpayer has increased his wealth annually over a period of several consecutive years. If the IRS can prove that a taxpayer's total expenditures exceeded his reported annual income in several years, the IRS has established one of the three elements of income tax evasion: that the taxpayer understated his income on which a tax was due and owing.[1]

---

1 In proving the crime of income tax evasion the government must prove the three elements of the crime: (1) that an additional tax was due and owing, United States v. Schenck, 126 F.2d 702 (2d Cir.), *cert. denied,* 316 U.S. 705 (1942); Gleckman v. United States, 80 F.2d 394 (8th Cir. 1935); (2) that an attempt was made to evade or defeat the tax, O'Brien v. United States, 51 F. 2d 193 (7th Cir.), *cert. denied,* 284 U.S. 673 (1931); and (3) that the attempt was willful, United States v. Murdock, 290 U.S. 389 (1933).

The IRS uses the net worth computation in the prosecution of cases when books and records necessary for calculating a taxpayer's income and expenses are unavailable. The Supreme Court of the United States has upheld the use of the net worth technique in criminal tax evasion cases.[2] The IRS's net worth computation is based on the following formula:

Line Number		
1.	Taxpayer's Net Worth-12/31/81	$ 257,000
2.	Taxpayer's Net Worth-12/31/80	- 146,000
3.	Increase in Net Worth in 1981	$ 111,000
4.	Add: Living Expenses (not included above)	+ 35,000
5.	Total Income	$ 146,000
6.	Less: Non-taxable Sources of Income	- 26,000
7.	TAXABLE INCOME	$ 120,000
8.	Less: Income Reported in Return	- 32,000
*	UNREPORTED INCOME	$ 88,000

The IRS net worth formula is usually applied to two or more prior consecutive years in order to show a pattern of illegality. As used by the IRS, the formula has no application in the investigation or prosecution of non-tax financial crimes. The necessity to credit the taxpayer for "non-taxable income" (line 6 in the above formula) makes the computation highly complex. Thus, the sophisticated nature of "non-taxable income" adjustments-the non-taxable portion of capital gains, deferred income, depreciation, etc.-requires that investigators and prosecutors have a sufficiently firm grasp of tax law to identify transactions that need an adjustment and later explain the adjustments to the jury during trial.

Stripped of its tax law complexities, a modified version of the IRS net worth formula can be applied in the investigation and prosecution of non-tax financial crimes. The formula, in its modified form, can be used to corroborate other evidence of a financial crime, thus overcoming the one-on-one dilemma. The modified computation is based on the following formula:

---

2 Holland v. United States, 348 U.S. 121 (1954); Friedberg v. United States, 348 U.S. 142 (1954); Smith v. United States, 348 U.S. 147 (1954); United States v. Calderon, 348 U.S. 160 (1954).

Line Number		
1.	Investigative Subject's Net Worth — 12/31/81	$ 257,000
2.	Investigative Subject's Net Worth — 12/31/81	<u>-146,000</u>
3.	Increase in Net Worth in 1981	$ 111,000
4.	Add: Living Expenses (not included above)	<u>+ 35,000</u>
5.	Total Expenditures	146,000
6.	Less: Legitimate Sources of Income	<u>- 58,000</u>
	EXPENDITURES MADE WITH FUNDS FROM ILLEGITIMATE OR	
7.	ILLEGAL SOURCES	$ 88,000

Note that the above computation, through Line 4, is exactly the same as the IRS computation.

Beginning with Line 5, however, the complexities of the IRS computation (regarding non-taxable sources of income) have been eliminated. There is no longer any reference to income taxes. The sole purpose of the above modified net worth formula is to: (1) determine total expenditures of an individual and not his total income (Line 5); and (2) to compare the individual's total expenditures to his legitimate sources of available funds (Line 6). If, as in the above illustration, the individual's total expenditures exceeded his funds available from legitimate sources, the government has strong corroboration for other evidence of the financial crime, and the one-on-one problem is solved.

In a series of conferences and training seminars over the past ten years, I have presented the modified net worth formula to countless numbers of auditors, criminal investigators, and prosecutors from cities all over the world. Employing comparative schedules similar to those illustrated in this article, I have demonstrated not only the relative simplicity of the modified formula, but also its applicability to the detection, investigation and prosecution of non-tax financial crimes. During my presentations I have stressed that the modified formula facilitates the investigation of white collar crimes, including political corruption cases and racketeering violations. Moreover, it requires very little understanding of tax law, since the formula has been stripped of its tax complexities. And finally, the modified formula provides admissible circumstantial evidence, useful in corroborating other evidence of the particular financial crime.

III. A Test of the Modified Net Worth Formula:

People v. Tempera

The modified net worth formula is applicable to fraud, waste, and abuse cases. Due to Suffolk County, New York District Attorney Patrick Henry's willingness to commit investigative and prosecutorial resources to a lengthy investigation and subsequent trial, the formula has successfully survived an actual test.

In the fall of 1981, Suffolk County Assistant District Attorney James O'Rourke and Assistant District Attorney Mark Cohen were faced with a classic one-on-one dilemma. The Suffolk County Commissioner of Labor was under indictment for multiple charges of perjury resulting from his denials, before a county grand jury, that he had received kickbacks from the recipients of CETA grants which he had approved.[3]

The prosecutors recognized the difficulties inherent in convincing a jury "beyond a reasonable doubt" that a public official with no criminal record received kickbacks, when the primary evidence of these kickbacks was the uncorroborated testimony of those who allegedly paid him. But investigators Steve Drielak and Steve Enoch, employed by the Suffolk County District Attorney's office, under the guidance of prosecutors O'Rourke and Cohen, had gathered considerable information concerning the defendant's expenditures over the past several years, the same years that the defendant was allegedly "on the take." With this information, O'Rourke decided to offer into evidence an array of documents concerning the defendant's expenditures. The purpose of the evidence was to show that the defendant was spending more money each year than he had available from *legitimate* sources, thereby creating an inference that he must have had an *illegitimate* source of funds.

---

3 For affirmance of the trial court's decision, see People v. Tempera, 462 N.Y.S.2d 512 (1983). The prosecution is documented in the following newspaper articles from Newsday: Jan. 29, 1982, at 3; Feb. 9, 1982, at 19; Feb. 11, 1982, at 17; Feb. 19, 1982, at 12; March 11, 1982, at 23; May 22, 1982, at 3.

After being qualified as an expert witness, I testified as to the impact or effect of the evidence of the defendant's expenditures. I was able to demonstrate that the defendant expended substantially more money than he had available from legitimate sources over a period of four years, the same years that he was allegedly "on the take."[4]

Accordingly, the prosecution was able to offer the jury corroboration of the direct evidence of payments to the defendant, thereby enhancing the credibility of the witnesses who paid him. Following the guilty verdict, several jurors remarked to the press that the "net worth" evidence was the deciding factor during their lengthy deliberations.[5]

IV. Admissibility of the Net Worth Corroborative Evidence

While the use of the net worth concept in income tax evasion cases has been sustained by the Supreme Court,[6] in *Tempera* the admissibility of net worth evidence as *corroboration* of other evidence was at issue. In convincing the court that evidence concerning the defendant's "net worth" was properly admissible, the prosecutors in *Tempera* stressed that such evidence has been applied and approved as probative circumstantial evidence in numerous cases concerning crimes other than tax evasion.[7] For example, in two leading narcotics cases the United States Court of Appeals for the Second Circuit approved the prosecutions' use of net worth evidence to corroborate other evidence of the substantive offenses. In *United States v. Barnes*,[8] the court sustained the admissibility of the defendants' tax returns which listed large

---

4 *See* Newsday, Feb. 19, 1982, at 12. The use of the net worth tactic "will be one of the biggest issues" on appeal, according to Tempera's attorney. Newsday, March 11, 1982, at 23.

5 *See* Newsday, March 11, 1982, at 23.

6 *See* note 2 *supra* and accompanying text.

7 It has been used in narcotics prosecutions, see, e.g., United States v. Barnes, 604 F.2d 121, 147 (2d Cir. 1978), *cert. denied*, 446 U.S. 907 (1980); United States v. Hinton, 543 F.2d 1002, 1012-13 (2d Cir.), *cert. denied*, 429 U.S. 980 (1976); United States v. Tramunti, 513 F.2d 1087, 1105 (2d Cir.), *cert. denied*, 423 U.S. 832 (1975); United States v. Falley, 489 F.2d 33, 38-39 (2d Cir. 1973); in robbery cases, see, e.g., United States v. Pensinger, 549 F.2d 1150, 1152 (8th Cir. 1977); United States v. Cavallino, 498 F.2d 1200, 1204-06 (5th Cir. 1974); United States v. Jenkins, 496 F.2d 57 (2d Cir. 1974), *cert. denied*, 420 U.S. 925 (1975); and in larceny cases, *see, e.g.,* United States v. O'Neal, 496 F.2d 368, 370-71 (6th Cir. 1974); United States v. Amerine, 411 F.2d 1130, 1131-32 (6th Cir. 1969); Leonard v. State, 22 So. 564 (Ala. 1897); Commonwealth v. Burnes, 182 A.2d 232, 237 (Pa. Super. Ct. 1962), *cert. denied*, 371 U.S. 948 (1963); Commonwealth v. Montgomery, 52 Mass. (11 Metc.) 534, 537 (1846).

8 604 F.2d 121 (2d Cir. 1978), *cert. denied*, 446 U.S. 907 (1980).

amounts of income under the headings of "other" and "miscellaneous."[9] "Not only was [this evidence] probative of the conspiracy and the substantive counts," said the Second Circuit, "but, as to Barnes, it was offered to show an element of the offense of conducting a 'continuing criminal enterprise,' 21 U.S.C. § 848, i.e., that the defendant obtained 'substantial income or resources' from the enterprise."[10] In *United States v. Hinton*[11] the court approved admission of evidence that the defendants had failed to file tax returns. The court explained that this evidence was offered in conjunction with other evidence demonstrating that the defendants had made large expenditures during the years of their alleged narcotics conspiracy.[12] Thus, "the Government's purpose was to negate the existence of any legitimate source for the money they had expended."[13]

Paramount to the prosecutors' argument for admissibility of the net worth evidence in *Tempera*, however, was the precedent from several corruption cases in which evidence of concealed wealth has been admitted. Like the *Tempera* case, both *United States v. Kenny*[14] and *People v. Connolly*[15] involved bribes and kickbacks.

In *United States v. Kenny*,[16] a case involving Hobbs Act extortion (18 U.S.C. § 1951), conspiring to defraud the United States (18 U.S.C. § 371), and Travel Act violations (18 U.S.C. § 1952), the trial court properly admitted $700,000 in bearer bonds, $50,090 in currency, and testimony concerning $1,200,000 in bank accounts. Despite the lack of a direct nexus between the funds and the alleged crimes, the Third Circuit affirmed the admission of this circumstantial evidence of excessive unexplained wealth where there was proof that the

---

9 604 F.2d at 147.

10 *Id.*

11 543 F. 2d 1002 (2d Cir.), *cert. denied,* 429 U.S. 980 (1976).

12 543 F.2d at 1012.

13 *Id.* at 1012-13. The court stated,
> The [trial] court so charged the jury as to the evidentiary use of the returns and explained that the jurors could in their discretion infer from the appellants' failure to file returns that they had no bona fide source of income upon which they could have drawn to make their large purchases.

Id. at 1013. The Second Circuit addressed the potential prejudicial effect of the net worth evidence in both *Barnes* and *Hinton*. Barnes, 604 F.2d at 147 ("If there was any prejudice stemming from the Government's use of the tax returns, it was of defendants' own making"); *Hinton,* 543 F.2d at 1013.

14 462 F.2d 1205 (3d Cir.), *cert. denied,* 409 U.S. 914 (1972).

15 253 N.Y. 330, 171 N.E. 393 (1930).

16 462 F.2d 1205 (3d Cir.), *cert. denied,* 409 U.S. 914 (1972).

kickbacks in question were made in cash.[17] The classic conspiracy case of *People v. Connolly*[18] involved the Borough President of Queens County and various participants in a scandalous sewer project. In *Connolly*, the Court of Appeals of New York sustained the admission of evidence concerning defendants' financial transactions and bank accounts, explaining that this evidence was "competent upon the question of motive and to show sudden enrichment."[19]

These cases establish that net worth evidence is properly admissible in cases, like *Tempera*, involving financial crimes other than tax evasion. The net worth analysis provides probative circumstantial evidence which corroborates other evidence of the substantive crimes.

V. Conclusion

Cases involving fraud, waste, and abuse have proliferated in recent years, as have white collar crimes generally. Correspondingly, problems associated with one-on-one, uncorroborated testimony have increasingly plagued criminal investigators, prosecutors, defense attorneys, and the courts. A modified application of the IRS net worth formula can solve the one-on-one dilemma by providing admissible, circumstantial evidence of an individual's expenditures in excess of his legitimate sources of funds.[20] This evidence can corroborate other evidence of the substantive offense, corroboration often vital to the prosecution of financial crimes.

---

17 *See* 462 F.2d at 1219-25.

18 253 N.Y. 330, 171 N.E. 393 (1930).

19 *Id.* at 342, 171 N.E. at 397. The court stated,
> During the period when Phillips was fraudulently attracting over $3,000,000 from the contractors which ultimately was paid by the city, and Connolly was in possession of over $145,000 more than his salary, Moore deposited in a bank over $60,000 more than his salary, over $52,000 of which sum was deposited in cash . . . The same reasons that made evidence of Connolly's transactions competent, made evidence of Moore's bank account competent.

Id. at 341-42, 171 N.E. at 397.

20 1 J. WIGMORE, A TREATISE ON THE ANGLO-AMERICAN SYSTEM OF EVIDENCE IN TRIALS AT COMMON LAW §§ 88, 89 & 154 (3d ed. 1940).

Appendix B

Form **4789**
(Rev. December 1985)

Department of the Treasury
Internal Revenue Service

Currency Transaction Report

▶ File a separate report for each transaction.   ▶ Please type or print.
▶ For Paperwork Reduction Act Notice, see page 3.
(Complete all applicable parts—See instructions)

OMB No. 1545–0183
Expires: 10-31-88

If amended report, see instructions and check here . . . . . ▶ ☐

Part I   Identity of individual who conducted this transaction with the financial institution

1 If multiple individuals involved, see instructions and check here . . . . ▶ ☐

2 Last name	3 First name	4 Middle initial	5 Social security number

6 Address (number and street)	7 Occupation, profession, or business

8 City	9 State	10 ZIP code	11 Country (if not U.S.)

12 Method used to verify identity: **a** Describe ▶
   b Issued by ▶   **c** Number ▶
13 Reason items 2-12 are not completed: **a** ☐ Armored car service (enter name) ▶
   b ☐ Mail deposit/shipment   **c** ☐ Night deposit or ATM transaction   **d** ☐ Multiple transactions (see instructions)

Part II   Individual or organization for whom this transaction was completed

14 If multiple individuals or organizations are involved, see instructions and check here . . . . ▶ ☐

15 Individual's last name	16 First name	17 Middle initial	18 Social security number

19 **a** Name of organization	**b** Check if: **(1)** ☐ broker/dealer in securities, or **(2)** ☐ financial institution (see instructions)	20 Employer identification number

21 Address (number and street)	22 Occupation, profession, or business

23 City	24 State	25 ZIP code	26 Country (if not U.S.)

Part III   Customer's account number(s) affected by transaction

27 **S** ☐ Savings ▶ . . . .   **T** ☐ Securities ▶ . . . .   **H** ☐ CD/Money market ▶ . . . .
   C ☐ Checking ▶   **L** ☐ Loan ▶   **O** ☐ Other (specify) ▶

Part IV   Type of transaction. Check applicable boxes to describe transactions

28 ☐ Currency exchange (currency for currency)

29 CASH IN: **F** ☐ CD/Money market purchased | 30 CASH OUT: **R** ☐ CD/Money market redeemed
   D ☐ Deposit   **H** ☐ For wire transfer | **C** ☐ Check cashed   **U** ☐ From wire transfer
   G ☐ Security purchased   **A** ☐ Receipt from abroad | **T** ☐ Security redeemed   **B** ☐ Shipment abroad
   P ☐ Check purchased   **K** ☐ Other cash in (specify) ▶. . . . . . . | **W** ☐ Withdrawal   **Y** ☐ Other cash out (specify) ▶. . . . . . .

31 Total amount of currency transaction (in U.S. dollars). ▶ $	32 Amount in Item 31 in $100 bills or higher $	33 Date of transaction (month, day, and year)

34 If other than U.S. currency is involved, please furnish the following information: **a** Exchange made ☐ for or ☐ from U.S. currency

b Currency name	**c** Country	**d** Total amount of each foreign currency (in U.S. dollars) . . ▶ $

35 If a check or wire transfer was involved in this transaction, please furnish the following information (see instructions):

a If more than one check or wire transfer is involved, see instructions and check here . . . . ▶ ☐

b Date of check or wire transfer	**c** Amount of check or wire transfer (in U.S. dollars) $	**d** Payee

e Drawer of check	**f** Drawee bank and MICR number

Part V   Financial institution where currency transaction took place

36 Check applicable box to indicate type of financial institution   **a** ☐ Bank (enter code number from instructions here) ▶ . . . .
   b ☐ Savings and loan association   **c** ☐ Credit union   **d** ☐ Security broker/dealer   **e** ☐ Other

37 Name of financial institution	38 Employer identification number

39 Address (number and street)	40 Social security number

41 City	42 State	43 ZIP code	44 MICR number

Sign Here ▶

45 Signature (preparer)	46 Title	47 Date
48 Type or print preparer's name	49 Approving official (signature)	50 Date

Form 4789 (Rev. 12-85)

Page **2**

Multiple Transactions

(Complete applicable parts below if box 1, 14, or 35a on page 1 is checked)

Part I Continued—Complete if box 1 on page 1 is checked

2 Last name	3 First name	4 Middle initial	5 Social security number

6 Address (number and street) | **7** Occupation, profession, or business

8 City	9 State	10 ZIP code	11 Country (if not U.S.)

12 Method used to verify identity: **a** Describe ▶

b Issued by ▶   **c** Number ▶

2 Last name	3 First name	4 Middle initial	5 Social security number

6 Address (number and street) | **7** Occupation, profession, or business

8 City	9 State	10 ZIP code	11 Country (if not U.S.)

12 Method used to verify identity: **a** Describe ▶

b Issued by ▶   **c** Number ▶

Part II Continued—Complete if box 14 on page 1 is checked

15 Individual's last name	16 First name	17 Middle initial	18 Social security number

19 a Name of organization | **b** Check if: **(1)** ☐ broker/dealer in securities, or **(2)** ☐ financial institution (see instructions) | **20** Employer identification number

21 Address (number and street) | **22** Occupation, profession, or business

23 City	24 State	25 ZIP code	26 Country (if not U.S.)

15 Individual's last name	16 First name	17 Middle initial	18 Social security number

19 a Name of organization | **b** Check if: **(1)** ☐ broker/dealer in securities, or **(2)** ☐ financial institution (see instructions) | **20** Employer identification number

21 Address (number and street) | **22** Occupation, profession, or business

23 City	24 State	25 ZIP code	26 Country (if not U.S.)

Part IV Continued—Complete if box 35a on page 1 is checked

35 b Date of check or wire transfer	c Amount of check or wire transfer (in U.S. dollars) $	d Payee

e Drawer of check	f Drawee bank and MICR number

35 b Date of check or wire transfer	c Amount of check or wire transfer (in U.S. dollars) $	d Payee

e Drawer of check	f Drawee bank and MICR number

Form **8300**
(Rev. August 1988)
Department of the Treasury
Internal Revenue Service

Report of Cash Payments Over $10,000 Received in a Trade or Business

▶ Please type or print.

OMB No. 1545-0892
Expires: 12-31-88

Part I Identity of Individual Conducting the Transaction

Last name	First name	M.I.	Social security number

Number and street	Passport number	Country	Alien registration number	Country

City	State	ZIP code	Country (if not U.S.)	Other identifying data (Specify)

Part II Individual or Organization for Whom This Transaction Was Completed

Individual's last name	First name	M.I.	Social security number

Name of organization	Employer identification number	Passport number	Country

Number and street	Business or occupation	Alien registration number	Country

City	State	ZIP code	Country (if not U.S.)	Other identifying data (Specify)

Part III Description of Transaction and Method of Payment

1 Amount of cash received . . . $ **2** Amount in item 1 in $100 bills . . . $

3 Nature of transaction:

Description of property or service

  a ☐ personal property purchased . . . .

  b ☐ real property purchased . . . .

  c ☐ personal services provided . . . .

  d ☐ business services provided . . . .

  e ☐ intangible property purchased . . . .

  f ☐ debt obligation paid . . . .

  g ☐ exchange of cash . . . .

  h ☐ escrow or trust funds . . . .

  i ☐ other (specify) ▶

4 Method of payment by customer:

  a ☐ Paid with U.S. currency or coin

  b ☐ Paid with foreign currency (describe)

5 Date paid

Part IV Business Reporting This Transaction

Name of reporting business	Identification number (EIN or SSN)

Street address	Nature of your business

City	State	ZIP code	

Under penalties of perjury, I declare that the information I have furnished above, to the best of my knowledge, is true, correct, and complete.

Sign ▶
Here

____
(Authorized Signature—See Instructions)   (Title)   (Date)

For Paperwork Reduction Act Notice, see page 2.   Form **8300** (Rev. 8-88)

Currency Transaction Report by Casinos

Form 8362
(January 1986)
Department of the Treasury
Internal Revenue Service

File a separate report for each transaction. Please type or print.

(Complete all applicable parts—see instructions)

OMB No. 1545-0906
Expires: 12-31-87

Part I — Individual or Organization for Whom This Transaction Was Completed

Individual's last name	First name	Middle initial	Social security number
Name of organization	Employer identification number (EIN)	Passport number	Country
Number and street	Business or Occupation	Alien registration number	Country
City	State	ZIP code	Country (if not U.S.)	Driver's permit (number and state)

Part II — Identity of Individual Conducting the Transaction (Complete only if an agent conducts a transaction for the person in Part I)

Last name	First name	Middle initial	Social security number
Number and street	Passport number	Country	Alien registration number	Country
City	State	ZIP code	Country (if not U.S.)	Driver's permit (number and state)

Part III — Patron's Account or Receipt Number ▶

Part IV — Description of Transaction. If more space is needed, attach a separate schedule and check this box ☐

1 Nature of transaction (check the applicable boxes)

  a ☐ Currency exchange (currency for currency)

  b CASH IN
    (1) ☐ Deposit (front and safekeeping) (3) ☐ Check purchased (see item 6 below) (5) ☐ Collection on account
    (2) ☐ Chips purchased (4) ☐ Wire transfer of funds (6) ☐ Other cash in ______ (specify)

  c CASH OUT
    (1) ☐ Withdrawal of deposit (front and safekeeping) (3) ☐ Chips redeemed (5) ☐ Other cash out ______ (specify)
    (2) ☐ Check cashed (see item 6 below) (4) ☐ Credit advance

2 Total amount of currency transaction (in U.S. dollars) $	3 Amount in item 2 in $100 bills or higher $	4 Date of transaction (month, day, and year)

5 If other than U.S. currency is involved, please furnish the following information:

Currency name	Country	Total amount of each foreign currency (in U.S. dollars) $

6 If a check was involved in this transaction, please furnish the following information (See instructions):

Date of check	Amount of check (in U.S. dollars) $	Payee of check
Maker of check		Drawee bank and city

Part V — Casino Reporting the Financial Transaction

Name	Identifying number (EIN)
Number and street	
City	State	ZIP code

Sign Here

▶ ______ (Casino employee who handled the transaction) (Title) (Date)

▶ ______ (Casino official reviewing and approving the Form 8362) (Title) (Date)

For Paperwork Reduction Act Notice, see page 2.   Form **8362** (1-86)

<table>
<tr><td>

Department of the Treasury

TD F 90-22.1 (4-90)

SUPERSEDES ALL PREVIOUS EDITIONS

</td><td>

**REPORT OF FOREIGN BANK
AND FINANCIAL ACCOUNTS**
For the calendar year 19
Do not file this form with your Federal Tax Return

</td><td>

Form Approved: OMB No. 1505-082
Expiration Date: 2/93

</td></tr>
</table>

This form should be used to report financial interest in or signature authority or other authority over one or more bank accounts, securities accounts, or other financial accounts in foreign countries as required by Department of the Treasury Regulations (31 CFR 103). You are not required to file a report if the aggregate value of the accounts did not exceed $10,000. Check all appropriate boxes SEE INSTRUCTIONS ON BACK FOR DEFINITIONS File this form with Dept. of the Treasury, P O Box 32621 Detroit, MI 48232.

1. Name (Last, First, Middle)	2. Social security number or employer identification number if other than individual	3. Name in item 1 refers to
		☐ Individual
4. Address (Street, City, State, Country, ZIP)		☐ Partnership
		☐ Corporation
		☐ Fiduciary

5. ☐ I had signature authority or other authority over one or more foreign accounts, but I had no "financial interest" in such accounts (see Instruction J). Indicate for these accounts:

(a) Name and social security number or taxpayer identification number of each owner ________________

____

(b) Address of each owner ________________

____

(Do not complete item 9 for these accounts)

6. ☐ I had a "financial interest" in one or more foreign accounts owned by a domestic corporation, partnership or trust which is required to file TD F 90-22.1. (See Instruction L). Indicate for these accounts:

(a) Name and taxpayer identification number of each such corporation, partnership or trust ________________

____

(b) Address of each such corporation, partnership or trust ________________

____

(Do not complete item 9 for these accounts)

7. ☐ I had a "financial interest" in one or more foreign accounts, but the total maximum value of these accounts (see instruction I) did not exceed $10,000 at any time during the year. (If you checked this box, do not complete item 9).

8. ☐ I had a "financial interest" in 25 or more foreign accounts. (If you checked this box, do not complete item 9.)

9. If you had a "financial interest" in one or more but fewer than 25 foreign accounts which are required to be reported, and the total maximum value of the accounts exceeded $10,000 during the year (see instruction I), write the total number of those accounts in the box below: Complete items (a) through (f) below for one of the accounts and attach a separate TD F 90-22.1 for each of the others. Items 1, 2, 3, 9, and 10 must be completed for each account.

Check here if this is an attachment. ☐

(a) Name in which account is maintained	(b) Name of bank or other person with whom account is maintained
(c) Number and other account designation, if any	(d) Address of office or branch where account is maintained

(e) Type of account. (If not certain of English name for the type of account, give the foreign language name and describe the nature of the account. Attach additional sheets if necessary.)

☐ Bank Account   ☐ Securities Account   ☐ Other (specify)

(f) Maximum value of account (see instruction I)

☐ Under $10,000   ☐ $10,000 to $50,000   ☐ $50,000 to $100,000   ☐ Over $100,000

10. Signature	11. Title (Not necessary if reporting personal account)	12. Date

PRIVACY ACT NOTIFICATION

Pursuant to the requirements of Public Law 93-579, (Privacy Act of 1974), notice is hereby given that the authority to collect information on TD F 90-22.1 in accordance with 5 U.S.C. 552(e)(3) is Public Law 91-508; 31 U.S.C. 1121; 5 U.S.C. 301, 31 CFR Part 103.

The principal purpose for collecting the information is to assure maintenance of reports or records where such reports or records have a high degree of usefulness criminal, tax, or regulatory investigations or proceedings. The information collected may be provided to those officers and employees of any constituent unit of the Department of the Treasury who have a need for the records in the performance of their duties. The records may be referred to any other department or agency of the Federal Government upon the request of the head of such department or agency for use in a criminal, tax, or regulatory investigation or proceeding.

Disclosure of this information is mandatory. Civil and criminal penalties, including under certain circumstances a fine of not more than $500,000 and imprisonment not more than five years, are provided for failure to file a report, supply information, and for filing a false or fraudulent report.

Disclosure of the social security number is mandatory. The authority to collect this number is 31 CFR 103. The social security number will be used as a means to ide

<table>
<tr><td colspan="2">Customs Use Only
Control No.
31 USC 5316; 31 CFR 103.23 and 103.25
Please Type or Print</td><td>DEPARTMENT OF THE TREASURY
UNITED STATES CUSTOMS SERVICE

REPORT OF INTERNATIONAL
TRANSPORTATION OF CURRENCY
OR MONETARY INSTRUMENTS</td><td>Form Approved
OMB No 1515-0079
This form is to be filed with the United States Customs Service

Privacy Act Notification
on reverse</td></tr>
</table>

PART I - FOR INDIVIDUAL DEPARTING FROM OR ENTERING THE UNITED STATES

1. NAME (Last or family, first and middle)	2. IDENTIFYING NO. (See instructions)	3. DATE OF BIRTH (Mo./Day/Yr.)
4. PERMANENT ADDRESS IN UNITED STATES OR ABROAD		5. OF WHAT COUNTRY ARE YOU A CITIZEN/SUBJECT?
6. ADDRESS WHILE IN THE UNITED STATES		7. PASSPORT NO. & COUNTRY
8. U.S. VISA DATE	9. PLACE UNITED STATES VISA WAS ISSUED	10. IMMIGRATION ALIEN NO. (If any)

11. CURRENCY OR MONETARY INSTRUMENT WAS: (Complete 11A or 11B)

A. EXPORTED		B. IMPORTED	
Departed From: (City in U.S.)	Arrived At: (Foreign City/Country)	From: (Foreign City/Country)	At: (City in U.S.)

PART II - FOR PERSON SHIPPING MAILING OR RECEIVING CURRENCY OR MONETARY INSTRUMENTS

12. NAME (Last or family, first and middle)	13. IDENTIFYING NO. (See instructions)	14. DATE OF BIRTH (Mo./Da./Yr.)
15. PERMANENT ADDRESS IN UNITED STATES OR ABROAD		16. OF WHAT COUNTRY ARE YOU A CITIZEN/SUBJECT?
17. ADDRESS WHILE IN THE UNITED STATES		18. PASSPORT NO. & COUNTRY
19. U.S. VISA DATE	20. PLACE UNITED STATES VISA WAS ISSUED	21. IMMIGRATION ALIEN NO. (If any)

22. CURRENCY OR MONETARY INSTRUMENTS DATE SHIPPED DATE RECEIVED	23. CURRENCY OR MONETARY INSTRUMENTS ☐ Shipped To ☐ Received From	NAME AND ADDRESS	24. IF THE CURRENCY OR MONETARY INSTRUMENT WAS MAILED, SHIPPED, OR TRANSPORTED COMPLETE BLOCKS A AND B. A. Method of Shipment (Auto, U.S. Mail, Public Carrier, etc.) B. Name of Transporter/Carrier

PART III - CURRENCY AND MONETARY INSTRUMENT INFORMATION (SEE INSTRUCTIONS ON REVERSE) (To be completed by everyone)

25. TYPE AND AMOUNT OF CURRENCY/MONETARY INSTRUMENTS	Value in U.S. Dollars	26. IF OTHER THAN U.S. CURRENCY IS INVOLVED, PLEASE COMPLETE BLOCKS A AND B. (SEE SPECIAL INSTRUCTIONS)
Coins ☐ A.	► $	A. Currency Name
Currency ☐ B.	►	
Other instruments (Specify Type) ☐ C.	►	B. Country
(Add lines A, B and C) TOTAL AMOUNT	► $	

PART IV - GENERAL - TO BE COMPLETED BY ALL TRAVELERS, SHIPPERS AND RECIPIENTS

27. WERE YOU ACTING AS AN AGENT, ATTORNEY OR IN CAPACITY FOR ANYONE IN THIS CURRENCY OR MONETARY INSTRUMENT ACTIVITY? (If "Yes" complete A, B and C) ☐ Yes ☐ No

PERSON IN WHOSE BEHALF YOU ARE ACTING ►	A. Name	B. Address	C. Business activity occupation or profession

Under penalties of perjury, I declare that I have examined this report, and to the best of my knowledge and belief it is true, correct and complete.

28. NAME AND TITLE	29. SIGNATURE	30. DATE

(Replaces IRS Form 4790 which is obsolete)

Customs Form 4790 (120384)

Appendix C

SAMPLE LETTER REQUESTING FINANCIAL INFORMATION
FROM THE DEPARTMENT OF THE TREASURY

Commissioner of Customs
Department of the Treasury
Attn: Reports Analysis Unit
Washington, D.C. 20229

OR:

Office of the Assistant Secretary (Enforcement)
Department of the Treasury
Washington, D.C. 20220

CONFIDENTIAL

Gentlemen:

The undersigned is Chief of Police for Capital City, State of
Columbia, and as such the chief law enforcement officer for this City.

Our Narcotics Asset Forfeiture Task Force is conducting an
investigation of JOHN A. DOE for suspected violations of Columbia state
laws prohibiting the manufacture of controlled substances and
transportation of such controlled substances within this state.
Specifically, our investigation concerns suspected violations of Title
23, Code of Columbia, Sections 201.201 and 301.301. The requested
information is material, relevant, and probative to our official
investigation of John A. Doe for these violations. [NOTE: IT IS NOT
NECESSARY TO PROVIDE THE DETAILS OF THE INVESTIGATION.]

The following information is pertinent to the suspect, JOHN A. DOE:

1. Name: John Albert Doe
2. Alias(es): Johnny Doe, Joe Doe, Joe Smith
3. Date of birth: June 1, 1952, New York, NY
4. Social Security No.: Unavailable
5. Md. drivers license no.: 00-123-456-7890

Please provide a printout of computer financial data to Deputy Chief
Richard Roe (telephone 200/555-1234), who is in charge of this
investigation.

Sincerely,

JOSEPH J. JONES
Chief of Police